THE KINGDOM OF
FREE MEN

THE KINGDOM OF
FREE MEN

BY

G. KITSON CLARK

*Reader in Constitutional History in the
University of Cambridge*

CAMBRIDGE

AT THE UNIVERSITY PRESS

1957

PUBLISHED BY
THE SYNDICS OF THE CAMBRIDGE UNIVERSITY PRESS

Bentley House, 200 Euston Road, London N.W.1
American Branch: 32 East 57th Street, New York 22, N.Y.

Printed in Great Britain at the University Press, Cambridge
(Brooke Crutchley, University Printer)

CONTENTS

PREFACE

THIS book is founded on a series of seven lectures which I delivered for the Divinity Faculty at Cambridge in the Michaelmas Term of 1955, as a course open to all members of the University. Since they were delivered from notes rather than from a completed manuscript, it has been necessary partially to rewrite them in more coherent form. In doing this I have made use of a certain amount of information which came to hand after the lectures were given, and have expanded some of the arguments which the shortness of the time available for each lecture had forced me to truncate. Nevertheless, my notes were full and what is published here is substantially the same as the lectures which I gave. In the circumstances, however, it seemed better to call the lectures 'chapters'.

I feel that I ought to apologize for dealing with topics on which I have no expert knowledge and with disciplines in which it will be clear that I have no expert skill. I am no theologian, no philosopher, no economist, and I pretend to no special knowledge of Eastern Europe, still less of the Far East. Yet I would plead that the importance of the subjects which I have tried to handle is of a nature to tempt a fool to rush in, indeed to give him something of a moral duty to do so, perhaps in the hope that angels will follow.

It seems to me that some of the gravest dangers which confront humanity spring from the large organized mass movements of fanatical opinion which are, perhaps increasingly, among the most potent weapons of modern politics. Much of the history of communism, of fascism, of the various nationalist movements at work in the world today, provide examples of what I mean, but the most notorious and terrible example is that of the Nazi movement in Germany. When the leaders of that movement had achieved power in the State, they used all the force at their disposal to impose their doctrine on all alike and to override the limitations which the standards of more old-fashioned creeds might have set upon action. Such books as Mr Wheeler-Bennett's *The Nemesis of Power. The German Army in Politics, 1918–45* (London, 1953), Mr Gerald Reitlinger's *The Final Solution. The Attempt to Exterminate the Jews of Europe, 1939–1945* (London, 1953), E. Crankshaw's *Gestapo. Instrument of Tyranny* (London, 1956) show clearly how complete was their success, how ambition, greed, moral uncertainty, fear or even a sense of duty led men of all sorts of traditions and positions to become the accomplices of the Nazis in deeds of an atrocity which earlier generations would not have thought to be credible. But many of those who so prostituted themselves seem to have been in fact only accomplices; however august their position, in the last analysis they were camp followers, attracted or compelled by the power of the movement, but not the source of its power. The source of power, the dynamic instrument which Hitler used to conquer the State and as a main source of energy when he controlled it, was the mass of fanatical opinion in the Nazi party itself, a body of opinion which he inspired, organized and on occasion betrayed. Without that he would surely have been nothing.

This body of opinion was truculent, dogmatic and very

emotional. It was fed on ideas which to minds that are not Nazi and not German seem unlikely to survive critical inquiry. This, however, mattered very little. For men and women, particularly for inexperienced and ignorant young men and young women, whose passions were involved, and for whom the Nazi movement seemed to provide all that life had to promise of hope and pride, here was a creed which was final and compulsive, worthy of their absolute sacrifice and devotion. For them any case that might have been urged against its teaching would not have been worth consideration, even if they had had a chance to consider it, and for them traditional ideas, older political traditions, must have seemed obsolete and without appeal, if not laughable or disgusting. So they yielded themselves up to be the docile and enthusiastic servants of tyranny, the motive power of one of the most dangerous forces that have ever threatened Europe.

Now the history of German opinion, and particularly of the opinion of German youth, between the wars was no doubt controlled by circumstances peculiar to itself. No doubt it was in a special way and in a special degree fated and tragic. Mr Leslie Paul's chapter on the 'Revolt of German Youth' in his *Annihilation of Man* (London, 1944) seems well worthy of consideration even by those who have not the leisure to read larger works, but it is much to be hoped that those who have expert knowledge of German life and history will instruct us further in this very important matter. It would, however, be very wrong to believe that the general problem which the history of Nazism suggests is confined to Germany. It is rather the result of conditions which are to be found in many countries today. In very many countries the formation, the manipulation and the direction of mass opinion are the keys to power, the machinery and techniques which enable men to use these keys are everywhere available, and the conditions which favour their use probably exist in most advanced societies.

It seems, for instance, possible that such movements of mass opinion are assisted by the rootlessness of modern urban life, and more certain that they receive force from the uncertainties and recurrent frustrations, as also possibly from the dull unrewarding routine, of modern economic conditions. It also seems to be very probable that the way is prepared for these movements by the education which the modern State extends to large numbers of its subjects and the limitations of that education. Young men and young women are often brought to a point at which they are no longer prepared to accept traditional orthodoxies; they can understand new ideas, but are not yet endowed with adequate powers, with the patience, the scholarship, the catholic sympathies and the knowledge, to criticize the ideas presented to them, or to place them in relation to other ideas and traditions. At the same time they have often been encouraged by the kind of education they have received to believe, not unnaturally, that they have a right to a way of life and a position, or at least opportunities to attain such a position, in the community which society, as traditionally organized, is unable or unwilling to afford to them. They are therefore apt to dislike all that seems to be compromised by association with the traditions of society.

All these things probably facilitate the exploitation of

the generosity, the need for hope, the pride and force of youth. They present a problem which is very difficult and deserves a more penetrating diagnosis than I can give. But one thing seems certain: the conditions which create it are not confined to Germany. Indeed those who were engaged in university education in Britain in the ten years between 1929 and 1939 will remember how communism took its toll of some of the best and most intelligent undergraduates. They were young men who desperately needed a faith and some programme which offered hope for themselves and for mankind. Secular hope in years which were shadowed from behind by the depression and from ahead by oncoming war was not easy to find; nor were they prepared to consider the case for the programmes of older political parties either of the right or the left, and they derided the religions of their forefathers. They were not always, indeed not often, personally unfriendly, but they were emotionally impermeable to argument. So they gave themselves recklessly, generously, credulously to a creed which was unworthy of them, and in due course might be ruthlessly exploited by men who were playing nakedly—for all but their dupes to see—the oldest game of all, the game of power politics. Conditions in Great Britain, and, despite their repeated claims to represent 'Youth', the relative smallness of the numbers affected, made anything like a mass movement impossible. In most cases this seems to have been a phase which men passed through and left behind; the worst that it did was to leave behind a certain number of individual personal tragedies; in other cases the experience may have done good and been enlightening for aught I know. Yet in the attitude revealed, in their emotionalism and their dogmatism, in the extreme harshness of the scepticism and cynicism with which these young men viewed traditional beliefs, and the unusual gullibility with which they accepted what was offered to them in the name of their new revelation, in fact in the habits of mind which led to the easy exploitation of youthful idealism by men of coarser moral fibre, the experience of these years may perhaps suggest some of the conditions of mind which make these mass movements of opinion the dangerous things that they are. It may not be too fanciful to say that they present as great a danger to humanity as the hydrogen bomb.

But these two dangers require very different treatment. The danger of the hydrogen bomb may perhaps be averted by stalemate. If two groups of potential enemies build up countervailing systems of armament, then it is possible that the balance may bring peace, that the chance of success will not suffice to tempt, and the certainty of receiving serious damage will be a strong argument to deter, a potential aggressor; for it must be remembered that it is not historically true to say that competitive armaments have always led to war. It is otherwise with the organization of massed bodies of opinion. Two masses of strongly held opinion, fanatical, ignorant, uncritical, constantly recharged from the batteries of propaganda and consciously directed against each other, are not likely to lead to peace between the nations, and they are very likely to lead to tyranny in their own bounds. The only answer to this danger is not to oppose like to like but to extend education still further, and to appeal from mass opinion to the individual intelligence, to increase the power and ability to criticize and analyse, and to encourage men and women to extend their knowledge and understanding of men and women in different historic situations with different historic traditions.

But by knowledge must be meant accurate knowledge, as far as it can be compassed, of all the facts, even when the facts are exceedingly unpleasant. Nothing could be more dangerous for humanity than to indulge in the moral indolence of an easy-going and ignorant tolerance. We can never afford to let bygones be bygones. In the last half-century very terrible things have happened; in the world of today very terrible things are still happening. It is of the first importance to find out what has been done, what is being done, and who have done it or are doing it, and to try to probe the motives and conditions that make it possible for men to do these things. The object of this is not to feed hate, or to encourage men and women to indulge in the luxury of moral indignation, nor yet to pass moral judgments on the agents of these actions, a task which, I believe, is beyond the capacity of human beings. The object is rather to try to understand the source of evil in order that we may perhaps guard against it or possibly eliminate it, to realize that the world is what it is and not what we would like it to be, and to stigmatize evil actions for what they are lest the moral currency of mankind be debased.

Inquiry into such matters will I believe reveal the terrible power of the forces of history over those who are at the same time their agents and their victims. But the inheritance from the past not only works for evil, it works for good as well. In particular we who live in the liberal democracies have inherited, not through our own merits but by good fortune and by reason of the merits of our ancestors, three things which if extended and made more effective can be of the greatest value to mankind. They are liberal institutions, the tradition of humanity and the Christian faith. It is, however, clear from all modern experience that traditional values can no longer simply rely on traditional authority for acceptance. As education develops they must increasingly rely on the inherent strength of their case and appeal not to inherited complacency, or to simple faith, but to the intellect. There are grave dangers in this situation, but it has to be accepted, and those who care for the self-respect and moral stature of mankind will, for all its dangers, be glad that it is as it is.

It is possible that at this moment conditions may be unusually favourable for securing the reconsideration of these inherited values. It is possible that in Europe at least the secular fanaticisms of the recent past may be burning themselves out, and that men may again, as in the eighteenth century, learn to look back on their wars of religion and see how fruitless and terrible they were. Certainly in Great Britain, during and since the war, a much more level-headed generation of young men and women has arisen who are more readily prepared to give a fair hearing to what is presented to them, even to the case for those things in which their grandparents believed. It is all-important that they should discuss these matters and form their judgments upon them, and it was my object in my lectures to stimulate such discussion. Certainly those who wish to consider many of the topics which I handle would be well advised to refer them to more expert authorities than myself, but at the least an amateur presentation may initiate debate, and it is possible that a university teacher should seek to do no more.

While preparing these lectures I have received much kind help from many people, so many in fact that it is impossible to name more than the principal ones. Professor Michael Oakeshott of the London School of Economics gave me advice on the definition of the totalitarian state. The Rev. H. M. Waddams of the Church of England Council of Foreign Relations gave me much help and information, and Colonel J. B. Barron very kindly read through my manuscript. Mr Douglas Woodruff, editor of *The Tablet*, gave me assistance, and the Catholic Truth Society sent me relevant pamphlets. The Rev. George Appleton, Mr Wallace C. Merwin, Mr B. D. Nicholls, the Rev. A. E. A. Sulston, Mr N. C. Pateman and Canon H. A. Wittenbach gave me very interesting information about China, and Dr W. O. Lewis and Mr Percy J. Buffard about Spain. My brother-in-law the Rev. Derwas Chitty has given me much assistance about the Orthodox Church. Sir Ernest Barker, Mr G. F. A. Best and the Rev. H. A. Williams, with great kindness, read through the lectures when in type. To all these people my very warm thanks are due; but in all cases I alone am responsible for the information presented and the views expressed; indeed, there are without doubt not a few statements and opinions in my lectures with which several of my advisers would most strongly disagree.

G. K. C.

August 1956

POSTSCRIPT

Since the earlier part of this Preface was written events in the world have moved swiftly, and they may seem to have rendered obsolete some of the problems advanced in it, or in the rest of the book. There has been the partial modification of the communist régime in Poland, the revolt in Hungary, its bloody suppression and the renewal of tension between Russia and the West. The renewal of tension does not touch my argument. The cold war is necessarily affected by passing events, contemporary needs and the individuals who may happen at any given moment to dominate the stage of history. At the moment it has become more virulent, in the near future it may very well become more virulent still, but in due course, unless fighting actually breaks out, there is likely to be another attempt to find a more peaceful *modus vivendi*. None of these secular changes affects the basic conflict of principle which divides the governments of the world, and it is no more, and no less, necessary to draw attention to what is fundamental in that conflict. However, something of profounder significance may be suggested by what has happened, what may even now be happening, in Europe. The revolt in Hungary, the movement even among communists which led to the changes in Poland, even the reports which have come through from time to time of the disillusion and discontent among young people and professional writers in Russia itself, may perhaps help to define the boundary beyond which the modern State, even the totalitarian State, can no longer control the mind and the spirit of man.

If that is so the matter is important indeed; it may well be the beginning of a new chapter in history. But in the present state of our knowledge it is more than usually necessary to be cautious, and to discriminate. Clearly conditions differ widely in different countries. In Hungary the official creed against which the revolt was directed was one imposed by a foreign power through the agency of a government of exceptional cruelty and ferocity, which was also the agent for the ruthless economic exploitation of the country for the benefit of the foreigner. In such a case a revolt both intellectual and physical was probable. In Poland the situation may have been in many ways comparable, but in Poland the hatred of Russia may well have been balanced in some degree by fear and hatred of Germany, a link upon which the Russian government may have known that it could rely. Even so, if what has happened in either case suggests limitations on the power of the modern State, with all its apparatus for propaganda and indoctrination, to control the minds of men, it must be remembered that in either case the State was encumbered by peculiar disadvantages. Obviously conditions are likely to be different elsewhere.

Conditions are likely, for instance, to be very different in those Asian or African countries where governments are using the mass movements of resurgent nationalism to consolidate their independence and to increase their force. This is perhaps particularly likely to be true of those countries, and there may come to be more of them, where nationalism makes use of the categories of communism or where communism exploits the passions of nationalism, and there is a large, poor, relatively unlettered but partially awakened mass to draw upon. The condition of opinion in Russia itself, or of some opinion in Russia itself, may be an interesting variant if it is true that some young people have become cynical about, some writers have reacted against, the wearisome reiterations of an endlessly dull and hidebound official orthodoxy. That certainly would suggest a limit to the power of the State to control the thought and the imagination of mankind. Even so it would be interesting to know how many even of those who are discontented still retain, without question, the basic assumptions about the nature of man, the shape of history or the condition of the non-communist world, which a communist upbringing has imposed upon them. Men may revolt against official propaganda and yet continue to bear on their minds the scars of official teaching; and, if that is so, their minds are still, in part at least, in the grip of the totalitarian State.

On all this more knowledge is needed. In fact if we are at the beginning of a new chapter the two most important problems it may raise may be: first, for how long can any State maintain a monopoly control over men's minds? And, second, if that control breaks down what takes its place? But there will certainly be a third question in it, carried over from what took place before this chapter started: for how long can the totalitarian States continue to control men's bodies? To that question at the moment the evidence gives no very encouraging answer, and it is a critical question. For however resilient the mind and spirit of man may prove to be, if the physical control remains in the hands of men who believe in totalitarian principles, or even of men who find it convenient to assume totalitarian principles, life will still be lived at discretion and the free development of the soul and intellect will never be secure.

But, whether we are at the beginning of a new chapter or no, I do not feel that even the secular issues raised in my book have become obsolete, or are likely to become obsolete for a very considerable period. I feel this the more because I am certain that what is most important is what is positive, and not what is negative. A revolution may be a very notable and significant event; but it is what comes after a revolution, or what is achieved without revolution, that controls the future. And to make the future secure for mankind there are needed not just a hatred of tyranny, or a rejection of official orthodoxies, but positive principles which may enable men to maintain their own freedom and will make them protect as their own the freedom of others, even of others with whom they disagree. It is to the consideration of such principles, and of their relation to Christianity, that I wish to turn men's minds.

Since writing the first part of the Preface I have acquired a new debt of gratitude—to my brother Commander E. Bidder Clark and to Dr L. Radzinowicz for their help with the Italian of Cardinal Ottaviani's speech, and also to the editor of *Osservatore Romano* for sending me the Italian version of the speech.

G.K.C.

April 1957

CHAPTER I

CHRISTIANITY AND THE GREAT DEBATE

THE subject which I wish to discuss is the relationship of 'Christian principles'—whatever these may be—to the great debate about forms of government which goes on without ceasing in the world at large. That is an issue of some importance for Christians, since in these matters an appeal to the sanctions of Christianity by contestants of sharply divergent opinions is inevitable, and natural. It may be legitimate; but the possibilities of mistake, and fraud, are so great that it is necessary for Christians to consider when, and with what results, their religion is rightly involved, and when it is not. It would, however, be impossible to consider this issue without propounding questions that concern everyone, whether he is a Christian or a non-Christian, whether he is interested in the claims made on the behalf of Christianity or profoundly indifferent to them; for they are questions to which any man or woman may be forced at some time to find some sort of answer, and an answer that might have to serve as a guide for conduct, an answer which in conceivable circumstances they might have to back with their life. I would like to suggest, therefore, that it would be as well for anyone to consider some of these matters calmly and systematically in the abstract before they can confront him confusedly and violently in the concrete.

For what is the great debate? It is concerned both with

questions of expediency and of absolute right. What is debated is not only what is the best and most efficient form of government, but what ends the State should serve, what form of government will best serve those ends, what rights the State possesses, what obligations rest upon the subjects of the State, and what are the limits of those obligations. It has in fact gone on continuously since human beings have been conscious of the way in which the communities in which they lived are organized. Sometimes it has meant the systematic comparison of constitutions and social structures; sometimes it has meant the mere rehearsal of deep-seated prejudices, with a cheer for this and a groan for that, to be answered by comparable noises from the other side, though in different places. Sometimes it has been flatly utilitarian, the simple comparison of different methods by which efficiency may be secured, and sometimes it has brought into question problems of the profoundest philosophical importance; indeed, it has often done this, for there is no system of ethics, however private and unworldly, which does not at some point have to consider the public obligations of the citizen.

For this reason, since Christianity came to be a force to be reckoned with, men engaged in it have very often appealed to what they have asserted are Christian principles to endorse their point of view; but since the issues have never been solely academic, they have also frequently appealed to force, either to armed force in war or to the gallows and the firing-squad where they could use those arguments on their opponents. But whatever its nature, the debate has always gone on, since man was advanced enough to think about these matters, and I think always will go on. A great deal of breath has been expended on it, much ink, and I am afraid not a little blood, but it will not come to a conclusion until human beings become completely content with their own condition and their neighbours' methods, a state of affairs which there seems to be no great reason to expect.

It has from time to time changed the vocabulary it uses and to some extent its subject-matter, and in the last thirty years its issues have come to seem to turn primarily on the difference between two apparently contrasting systems of government as severally practised in two groups of states into which the governments of the most advanced countries of the world have been very roughly distributed. Before the war these were normally called the democracies and the dictatorships, or in terms which I would prefer because I think they raise deeper problems, the democracies and the totalitarian States. The exigencies of war broke into this alignment since it brought about the alliance of Russia with the Western democracies, and a period of rather confused nomenclature developed, when that hard-pressed maid-of-all-work, the word 'democracy', was stretched to include any form of government in any country that was prepared to fight Germany or Japan. That confusion was, however, the result of the urgency of outward circumstances, and had little to do with systematic thought. When peace came in 1945, a new and much clearer alignment took place, along the line of the iron curtain. The debate was now between the democracies and the communist powers. The communist powers confused matters by using the term democracy for their forms of government; they called them 'people's democracies'. To Western publicists this was an abuse of the word, but possibly it made necessary a closer definition of the governments in the free world. Certainly it was claimed that the governments in the non-communist world were not only 'democracies', but that they embodied 'Western European' or 'liberal' traditions, or alternatively 'the Christian tradition'. This was of course not the first time that appeal had been made to the Christian tradition; it had been evoked in the struggle with Hitler. In that struggle there was good reason for such an appeal; there is possibly equally good reason for an appeal to Christianity in the struggle with communism; yet the use of the 'Christian tradition' and the 'liberal tradition' as alternative terms does present problems which I wish to discuss.

Nevertheless, in the period between 1945 and 1955, whatever difficulties the problems of nomenclature and this troublesome word 'democracy' may have offered, men engaged in the debate had little difficulty in making clear to what systems they were referring; after all, the governments of the world were divided by a sharply defined diplomatic frontier across which there was endless vituperation, the unceasing threat of war and on occasion actual armed aggression. There may be reason to hope that a more peaceful period is about to begin. However, if this is so, there may be a slurring of differences which will have its own dangers; for what is in question in the great debate is an ideological rather than a diplomatic frontier; not what states are aligned against each other, but two sharply contrasted views of the principles to be observed in the government of man.

For this reason, indeed on all counts, it is peculiarly necessary to define clearly what are the basic two principles of the parties to the debate as it now stands. The best names to give them are, probably, the 'liberal democracies' and the 'communist totalitarian States'. Nor is it difficult to enumerate which States come into either group: France, Belgium, Holland, the United States, Great Britain and the Scandinavian countries are among the liberal democracies, while Communist Russia and its satellites and Communist China are communist totalitarian States. However, in this terminology probably the most difficult, and probably the most important, words are 'liberal' and 'totalitarian', so the analysis must be pressed further and the word totalitarian so defined as to include Nazi Germany or Fascist Italy: States which were totalitarian without being communist.

Nowadays, I believe, a good many people hold that the principle of self-determination is the most appropriate touchstone with which to try governments; consequently it may seem that the best test of a liberal democracy is that it should possess representative government based on recurrent free elections protected by the secret ballot for the voters and all the other arrangements which have been designed to secure free discussion and choice. Only so, it will be said, is it certain that the will of the majority of the people is effectively and continuously expressed in the government of the State. There are, however, difficulties in using free elections by themselves as the test for a liberal State, or in relying too confidently on the principle of majority rule. Freedom of election is after all only one among many institutions which are designed to protect liberty in a liberal state; and the liberty which is to be secured, the rights which such institutions are designed to guarantee, must at times be those of groups and individuals who have not the remotest chance of ever securing a majority which is even sympathetic to them. Besides, in many countries, it is not always clear beyond a peradventure that the clumsy compromising methods of free election and parliamentary rule will in fact be those which most certainly ensure that the will of the majority will prevail; there are circumstances when it seems very probable that the will of the majority is most effectively put into force by a dictatorship. This is unfortunate, but the fact that we dislike the result does not destroy its validity. Indeed, it is hard to escape the belief that the government of Hitler in 1936 expressed the will of the majority of the German people at that moment more truly and decisively than could have been done by the manœuvres and compromises of any number of parliamentary politicians returned by a series of free but indecisive general elections. To discover, therefore, the essential differences of principle between the two groups of states it is necessary to look more closely at their characteristic institutions.

The basic principle in a liberal democracy is probably the rule of law, the principle that a human being ought as far as possible to live his life subject to a known law. This law ought to have been recognized from antiquity or passed by constitutional means before it is invoked in an individual case. It should pay respect to the inherent rights of men and women as men and women, and to those mysterious principles which are difficult to define

6

but more easy to recognize, the principles of justice. It must as far as possible be enforced by men who are not under the control of the power which directs the policy of the State, but who will take account only of the facts before them and of rules which are the same for all similar cases, and who will therefore not be swayed in any particular case by the administrative needs of the moment. For the object of the rule of law is to secure, as far as is possible, that men shall not live their lives at discretion, permitted or forbidden to do things, left at liberty or incarcerated, granted life or condemned to die, as suits the changing policy of the executive authority.

The rule of law is the substratum of all liberal society, for without it no individual right can be securely enjoyed. However, in all liberal societies men must enjoy, within reason, certain essential rights which the law must as far as is practicable secure. There must, for instance, be freedom of opinion, as far as that can be a reality; men must not be punished or handicapped for holding particular opinions, though they may be prevented from acting on their opinions if that will endanger the State. There must be freedom of access to information, opportunities for parents to educate their children in their beliefs, if that can be arranged; there must be freedom of utterance, subject, of course, to the rights of other persons not to be defamed, to the needs of public security and the public peace. There should be reasonable freedom of action, subject again, of course, to respect for the rights of others and public security. There should also be freedom of association, though not for such actions as might endanger the ordinary well-being of other members of the community. These and other liberties the laws and institutions of the liberal State must endeavour to secure, as far as such liberties can be secured by institutions and laws.

Such laws and institutions will not be needed, much less will they have any sacrosanct authority, in the totalitarian State. For such a state will undertake, or will reserve the right to undertake, to decide how a man is to vote, think, speak, educate his children and act. In the totalitarian State the subject can have no rights against the State; that statement, however, points to a difficulty. In a liberal democracy also the subject can have no rights against the State. In domestic matters at least, a liberal democracy must be, if it is to survive as an organized community, a sovereign State in which a law constitutionally passed and properly enforced must take effect, however unjust or intolerable it may seem to the individual. The common order, if it is to continue, may not be at the mercy of eccentric opinion or the vagaries of the particular conscience, while the battery of provisos, modifications and limitations which have to be recorded with any statement of any important public liberty establish the fact that no orderly community could continue to exist which allowed its subjects untrammelled liberty in any direction whatsoever. Neither in potential power, nor altogether in the use of power, can the liberal State differ absolutely from the totalitarian State.

Where the totalitarian State and the liberal State ought to differ absolutely is in intention. In the liberal democracies the intention ought to be to respect individual rights as far as possible, and it ought to be the object of the State so to organize matters that private men and women can make as many of their choices as is possible for themselves. The totalitarian State will have no such intention. It will desire as far as it can to make its subjects' choices for them, and, when a State is equipped with all the power that modern technique has provided for governments, that is very far indeed. Nor will a totalitarian State have any intention of respecting the rights of its subjects, for it will not believe that its subjects could have any rights which it would desire to respect, certainly no right to freedom of choice in any matter in which the State is interested.

This denial of individual right may be justified in a variety of ways. The rulers of the State may perhaps regard their subjects, or large groups of their subjects, as being less than human, and therefore as possessing no human rights; in Nazi Germany, for instance, a Polish labourer had no more rights than a cow or a pig, because a Pole was less than a human being. Or certain classes of the community may be regarded as inherently criminal and therefore as having forfeited human rights, as members of the old 'exploiting' classes have been at times considered to be outside the law in communist States. As a matter of fact a simpler and more universal justification for this denial of rights is available nowadays. It may be held that science has plainly established the fact that not even human beings have any power of free decision, and that, since science has also demolished the possibility that any source of transcendental right can exist, there really can be nothing to bother about. This, however, is rather too sweeping a hypothesis to be advanced openly, and the most common general justification for totalitarianism derives from the belief, often enough sincerely held, that all that is worth while for the human beings who are the subjects of a totalitarian State is in fact summed up in the purposes of that State. There is no need, therefore, to respect any individual intention which does not correspond with those purposes, no need to reserve from the control of the State any sphere of private decision out of respect for the personality of the subject. The State's demands on the subject may be total because it represents the totality of all that is valuable for mankind.

To be effective, however, such a belief must be based on an absolute certainty that the State does possess this monopoly of value. Any lingering belief that there exist any values of equal importance outside the operations of the State which the rulers of the State ought to consider in framing their demands on their subjects would limit the State's totality. Such certainty has, however, not proved hard to achieve, and were it questioned certain arguments could be used. It could be asserted, for instance, that the demands of the State were based on the clear findings of science, and that they represented the manifest needs of humanity at the present stage. Or it might be asserted by another type of ruler that they plainly represented the clearly revealed will of God.

All this, however, raises another and most important problem. If the theory of the totalitarian State is based upon certainty about essential values, is the theory of the liberal State necessarily based upon uncertainty, or accepted disagreement about them? Must one say that the liberal State does not intend to impose one view of truth, or one line of conduct, either because its members are in hopeless disagreement as to what is truth, or proper conduct, or are only agreed that there can never be absolute certainty on either head? Many of the enemies of the liberal State would assert that the answer to this question is 'yes', that this is both the reason for the existence of the liberal State and the cause of its weakness and moral confusion. Some of its friends would also be glad to answer 'yes', for there are those who believe that some decent scepticism about essentials is necessary, or at least that there must be a reasonable disagreement upon them, before men can be persuaded to tolerate each other's opinions. In fact, however, if this were the whole truth, if this were all there was to the theory of the liberal State, the situation would be dangerous indeed. Organized uncertainty would be a feeble weapon with which to fight organized certainty, for, as we shall see, it can be explicitly claimed that those who are certain of their opinions have a right to impose their views by methods which those who are uncertain have no right to use. Moreover, if freedom were based upon a purely negative principle, it would not be easy to limit in its name those demands for compulsion which the needs of efficiency and convenience, without much reference to absolute values, are constantly making.

In fact this is not, and cannot be, the whole truth. The members of a liberal State are necessarily agreed on two principles which they must regard as certainties. The first is that it is better for human beings, as far as is possible, to make their choices for themselves, and the second is that they have inherent rights as individuals. Without these two principles, compulsion would be just as tolerable a policy as liberty; it would simply be used as convenience directed. Now neither of these principles can be called a negative opinion; they are not begotten of uncertainty and hopeless disagreement. They are in fact very positive principles based upon highly disputable assumptions, and not easy to square with the facts of the world. To Christians in particular they present a peculiarly difficult problem, for can it in any circumstances be better for men and women not only to be free to choose to reject Christianity, but to choose to try to make others reject it? Can men possibly have the right to obscure the source of all right? There are those who without much hesitation would answer 'no'.

Yet it is upon these audacious presumptions about the nature of man and of his rights that the philosophy of the liberal State is founded; it is this which should direct its intention; and a comparison of the institutions and the conditions that prevail in the liberal States in the world at the present moment with what is to be found among the totalitarians shows that that intention, and the institutions, and the traditions through which it is conveyed, have very profound and important results for those who have the advantage of them. They are probably worth dying for.

It is, however, important not to exaggerate. These principles have a long history, they are enshrined in ancient institutions and enforced by valued traditions; but it is in the world of today that the liberal States have to exist. The terms of existence in that world will be the same for them as for the totalitarian States, and the contemporary atmosphere—that peculiar framework of ideas, assumptions and feelings which makes any historic period unique—is not likely to be entirely different on all points for civilized States existing at the same time. Moreover, the liberal States have been subjected to some of the reactions against old beliefs which have helped to make other States totalitarian.

For instance, the moral weakness of the old conception of freedom was that its full benefits were enjoyed by only a section of the population. Probably those benefits meant more to more people than is now usually believed, but the main fact is indisputable. There were many to whom poverty, economic dependence, ignorance and miserable conditions allowed little power of choice; while privilege and the power of wealth secured that legal and political rights existed for many only in the imaginations of orators, and a traditional acceptance of economic inequality obscured moral realities. No one denies these facts, in fact a great many people gain much moral satisfaction from constantly repeating them. What is more to the purpose, all civilized States are making vigorous efforts to remedy the conditions which were their cause. Not communist governments only, but all civilized governments are carrying through a social revolution. The work of education, rehousing, of the control of disease and of unemployment, is going busily forward, and must be continued, if all men and women are to have the share in life which they ought to have; and there is only one agent which can do much of this work. It is the government, or at least some public authority which utilizes the general compulsive power of the government. For this reason the most marked characteristic in all countries of the last fifty years of political development has been the increase, sometimes applauded, often enough detested, but always unceasing and apparently irreversible, of the powers of the State. Probably it is unavoidable, possibly it is the road to freedom, in the end: but before that end is reached this process does not with any certainty increase the freedom of choice of the individual or maintain much respect for private right.

Nor are the demands of social idealism the only cause for this increase in the concentration of power. It is made unavoidable nowadays by the necessities of life; an increasingly effective concentration of power is indeed the condition of survival for a modern advanced community. A modern community is confronted by three clamorous necessities: the needs of a population astronomically larger than anything that existed in the seventeenth and eighteenth centuries, the need to supply ever rising standards of life and the demands of an increasingly elaborate technology; and they may also have to face the demands of total war. To meet these necessities increasingly complex organizations have to be used with specialized parts subordinated to central control. It is a process which started with the development of factories when over a hundred years ago the hand-loom weavers were eliminated, and the first agent to be responsible for it was privately owned capital. But the primary reasons for this development were largely technological; they had little or nothing to do with ethical or ideological conceptions, or the way in which property was owned. The larger unit with its capital under concentrated control, and not diffusely distributed in the hands of individual craftsmen, was necessary for mass production, and mass production was necessary to provide the new multitudes of human beings with the goods that they needed if they were to maintain or improve their standards of life.

Those technological necessities continue to develop in every advanced country, whether its system is nominally free capitalist, socialist or communist. In many cases they have meant an increase in the size of the unit of production; the smaller factory has given place to the larger factory, the privately owned concern to the great company, the great company to the syndicate, the syndicate to the national undertaking. In Great Britain the full process can perhaps be best seen in the development of the organization for providing electrical power; private or locally controlled electricity companies in due course became organized in the national grid and then gave way to the Central Electricity Authority, while the supply of power is now to be supplemented by the National Atomic Authority from sources which could only have been developed by the public effort of the whole community. Other industries have not gone as far as this, but many of them have at least gone far enough to engulf the individual worker and manager. It may be a matter of controversy whether in fact the individual worker is better protected in this system of large units by free trade unions in a free capitalist society, or by the State under socialism, or by the classless society under communism, were such a system ever to emerge from the land of dreams; but the process which creates these large units can never become the subject of effective political controversy—it is too technical and it is too inevitable.

The results for the individual worker may in fact be more nearly the same in all types of society than controversialists on either side of the great debate would desire them to be. In many ways they are good. Certainly in countries like Great Britain and the United States the rewards of the individual worker have enormously increased above what they could have been if he had remained a private craftsman in a society of private craftsmen; in course of time his conditions of work have been greatly improved, while the development of automatic machines will probably make much of his work more intelligent and interesting, since it will become the skilled oversight of machines doing for him what was repetitive and soul-destroying. But however free the country, he will never be his own master again. On the contrary, as far as can be seen, more and more members of the population will have to fit into specialized positions in large undertakings, the control of which will necessarily be expert, complex and remote.

In non-industrial matters also, the very necessities of the case increasingly impose this technical control on the whole community. Again the process started in the nineteenth century. Possibly its first notable development was in the work of draining, providing water and controlling nuisances in overcrowded cities, and perhaps the most significant date is the year 1866 when 'the grammar of common legislation'—on public health—'acquired the novel virtue of the imperative mood'. Much of the impulse for this work came from social idealism, but it is not often sufficiently realized to what extent sheer necessity made collectivism unavoidable. The checking of cholera, typhus and fever was a necessary condition for the preservation of life in the cities of nineteenth-century Britain; it was not only needed to improve the lot of the poor. It was work which could only be done under the control of the expert, and that control was gradually extended into all departments of life, as in the work of providing clean food and clean milk, or controlling pests in agriculture. New inventions have enforced new forms of expert control, as for instance the invention of the motor car which has created the need for better engineered roads, more scientifically planned by authorities more centralized than the locally elected bodies who used to be charged with this duty, and it has created the need for more exacting discipline on the roads. In this century the brute necessities of two wars have developed the technique of social organization, economic control, the control of currency exchange, investment and consumption to an extent that before 1914 would not have seemed to be possible; and the powers that the State gains in war never seem to be completely relinquished when peace is achieved, whatever type of government may come into power, for to many of these matters the amateur excitements of party politics seem to be wholly irrelevant. In fact in a thousand and one ways, largely unnoticed, the expert and the technologist have extended their grasp on the community.

Much of this development has been undoubtedly beneficial, but all of it reduces freedom. In fact we live under a discipline of which our grandfathers never dreamed in their worst nightmares, and we can but speculate what will be the condition of our grandsons. We may welcome this tendency as the development of the spirit of order, or hate it as the road to serfdom, or be, with the crowd, indifferent, until we stub our feet on something peculiarly annoying; but there is very little sign that we can do much to delay it, or put it into reverse. Political battles have been fought over the extension of the power of the State, and it has been possible for certain controls like the rationing of food to be dispensed with for a time; moreover, parliamentary government can sometimes mitigate the way in which the administrative machine treats the ordinary man. But if the general results of the last fifty years are taken into review, it is clear that the changes of government make little difference to the increasing elaboration of the power of the State. It is made necessary by the need for social reform, but it is also unavoidable because in an increasingly complicated and artificial society more and more of life must be under the control of the technologist and the expert, if we are to live our lives on the only terms on which they are offered to us.

The domination of the technologist has not only its results in the organization of society, it has spiritual results as well. The words 'materialism' and 'determinism' are ugly equivocal words, but they cannot be neglected. Marxist-Leninist communism is unashamedly materialist and probably with some hesitation determinist as well; these factors in its theory contribute to the totalitarianism of the communist State. In the liberal democracies that theory is largely rejected, but men can be materialist without accepting any theory or thinking at all continuously about anything theoretical. In a society which depends so immediately on his efforts, it is natural and right that the prestige of the technologist should be great. He after all is the conjuror with the wonder box. Fate seems to be in his hands. There is naturally and rightly an increasing concentration on his problems, and more and more of the machinery of education must be diverted to supply him with technical assistants.

His ways of thought therefore may very well come to dominate the community. Yet it is unlikely that his thought and experience should disclose all that is important in life. It is probable that the methods of natural science both pure and applied taken as a whole are not sufficient to explore the whole of reality, and it seems certain that the exclusive application of a man's life to a few selected specialized problems of applied science will not yield a complete picture. But such experience does seem sometimes to suggest to the individual who has engaged in it that he has quite certainly answered questions which he has never properly asked; for he has never had time to consider the problems or weigh the experience which challenge the answers he is disposed to give. And in what he has never carefully considered and never deeply experienced, in art, philosophy and religion, may lie all grounds for belief in freedom of choice or in any claim for any general system of right or value for mankind. If the technologist makes our gods, they are likely to be tyrannical ones.

Thus, though the liberal democracies and the totalitarian states still stand far apart, it is possible that strong impersonal forces, the conditions of existence in the modern world, may be drawing them together till they more nearly resemble one another. If so, the movement does not tend to the extension of liberty.

Yet for all this the liberal democracies and the totalitarian States still stand very far apart. The difference between them forms much of the subject-matter for that noisy exchange of vituperation which men call the 'cold war'. Now the cold war and the great debate are not identical. The governing factor in the cold war is unavoidably diplomatic. It rises to a fury when diplomatic needs become pressing and dies away when there seems to be some chance of peace, though the differences of principle remain unchanged; for the frontier over which it is fought is unavoidably dictated by diplomatic needs and not primarily by ideological conceptions. However, the very existence of the cold war reminds us of something which men in my profession sometimes forget.

In the academic profession when we take account of the great debate we spend much time on the analysis and refutation of arguments, and the concoction of long lists of significant philosophers, whose systems in epitome we teach to the young. These are useful and respectable occupations appropriate to our calling, but they may lead to the belief that the matter can be worked out in the library without going out of doors. The ideas, however, that have moved humanity are of flesh and blood rather than ink and paper. If they were born in the library, they soon escaped to the market-place where it is often dangerous to analyse the other man's philosophy and normally quite useless to refute him. For the ideas in the market-place have normally become flesh by assuming to themselves the memories and hopes and hatreds of mankind; and often enough they have been married indissolubly to those powerful instinctive feelings which are the stuff of nationalism. We can know this if we can think at all honestly and objectively about the belief in freedom or liberal democracy as it exists in France or the United States or Great Britain. The same thing is also true of the other side.

When I was an undergraduate at Cambridge and working for the History Tripos on the subject which was then called political science, I used to be confronted by this difficulty. I could sometimes understand the arguments propounded by the exponents of what seemed to be the more extravagant political creeds, I could even imagine that men with sufficiently perverted ingenuity and ill-used leisure could have constructed them for some unknown ulterior purpose; what was beyond my understanding and imagination was that anyone could have believed in them. This was of course because I did not share the circumstances of the life of those who had done so, and did not know that, before I considered their ideas, I must try, however feebly, to recreate them. That task is, however, a primary necessity. When a man talks about some overriding will which transcends for him all the ordinary wishes of private men and has abolished any private right which ordinary individuals may have believed themselves to possess, it may well be that he does so, not because he has thought out a scheme which demands that conception, but because he feels, with passion, that this language precisely represents values which his experience has revealed to him. Not always, but very often, the totalitarian State is the sequel to a revolution. To its devotees there came from that revolution the wind which blew on their dry bones and made them men. That force is continued in the institutions which the revolution threw up and in the philosophy of which it made use, and these things contain for such men all that can be valuable in life, both for the children of the revolution and, as far as they can see, for any man of goodwill. For the sake of these things they are prepared to sacrifice anything and everyone, themselves and, without compunction, other men and women, for the idea that any human being has the right to oppose the cause, or do anything but serve its purposes, would not seem to them to be worth a moment's consideration.

Other passions than those of the revolutionary play on men's political theories; in some cases it may be difficult to diagnose them, but to present these ideas without the passions that give them life and validity is utterly to misunderstand them and tragically to underrate the full seriousness of the situation. Yet this is what we often do, though we should have had examples enough to preserve us from the error of exaggerating the importance of logic in the ideas that control mankind. For instance, from any intellectual standpoint Nazism is not only a degraded, it is a puerile creed; where it is not unintelligible neither fact nor logic can support it; yet this creed swept through one of the most highly educated nations in Europe and came near to wrecking civilization. Marxist-Leninist communism is both morally and intellectually superior to Nazism, but its logic is questionable, the history upon which it is based is indefensible, its claim to the support of science can only be maintained by imposing a severe discipline upon scientists, and its record contains matter at which any civilized man should shudder. Yet this creed has penetrated all countries, it has commanded the profoundest devotion, a devotion so absolute that men have been prepared gladly to accept savage punishment for obeying legitimate orders when the policy that they embodied became inconvenient to their masters. It is necessary to understand this devotion if we are to know where we stand.

In the great debate therefore not ideas alone are in conflict, but passions also, or rather ideas and passions indissolubly united. Passions beget violence, and are begotten by violence, and this has been a century of violence. In the last thirty years things have been done which are as bad as, or worse than, anything in recorded history, and what is most sinister is the fact that those who authorized them had neither repugnance nor any shame for what they did. They seem to have adopted a system of morality in which such actions are not condemned: so far can the passionately held idea carry man from what had been believed to be his natural instincts; or alternatively—the choice of opinion depends on your conception of man—so easily can a change in ideas destroy those principles upon which moderately humane conduct was based.

But this adds another complication. Violence comes to be answered by violence; indeed, if it is not to prevail and rule and ravage humanity, that may be the only effective answer. Yet even protective violence has its effect upon its agent. Whether we suffer, whether we resist, or whether we only observe, we shall indeed be affected by other men's violence. We are in fact watching a play in which we ourselves are actors, yet we are trying to judge it by the standards of something which stands outside its secular interests and passions.

Christianity is not of the world, but it is in the world. The Cross of Christ stands firmly planted in the rocky soil of Calvary, and whether they like it or not Christians must take up their parts in the earthly drama, not only as men but as Christians, or under the title of Christians. The results are sometimes tragic, or horrible, or even absurd. As is the case with other ideas, Christianity can also become fused with earthly passions; and as a result men do things in its name which are either absurdly remote from its spirit, or in horrible contrast to it. Or alternatively the practice of Christianity, or the working existence of Christian Churches, may come to seem inconvenient or even dangerous to the rulers of the darkness of this world, and Christians may be called to bear tragic witness to their creed. All this however leads to the subject of my next chapter, which is religious persecution in Europe since 1945.

CHAPTER II

RELIGIOUS PERSECUTION IN EUROPE SINCE 1945

RELIGIOUS persecution, that is, the persecution of religious people on account of their faith, not necessarily persecution by religious people to impose a rival faith, clearly raises in an acute and painful form the problem of the relation of Christianity to prevalent political systems. It is one of the issues of the great debate, but those who are persecuted may not have liberty to be concerned with those issues in general. It may not be open to them to say whether they approve as Christians of this or that type of régime, since they must be exclusively concerned with two rather more elementary questions, whether Christianity is to survive at all in a particular area, and whether Christian Churches are to be able to do the work there that it is their duty to do.

Of course it might be said that if men are brave enough neither issue ought ever really to be in doubt; but I am afraid that is too sanguine. I know the blood of the martyrs is said to be the seed of the Church, *sanguis martyrum semen ecclesiae*, and I think it is sometimes believed that courage and devotion will by their native force certainly defeat persecution. Alas, neither statement is always true. The blood of the martyrs may be the seed of the Church if not too much is shed for too long and there is opportunity for the harvest of their sacrifice to be reaped. If not, it is very possible that courage and devotion, however great, may not prevail. The fate of Christianity in seventeenth-century Japan, or for that matter of Protestantism in sixteenth-century Spain, suggests that if persecution goes on long enough, and is pressed far enough, it may very well be successful in the end.

Moreover, a Christian Church has other and more important tasks than that of pronouncing on the moral claims of the régime under which it happens to live. It must convey the sacraments to the faithful and confirm them in their belief, it must marry and baptize, it must guide the living and console the dying, it must instruct the young. It is not always open to a Christian bishop or Christian priest or minister to do what a journalist or politician may normally do, that is leave the country and continue the battle from elsewhere in comparative safety. Unless he can make other provision he must stay with his flock and perform his duty towards them, accepting for himself whatever is coming to them, and subjecting himself to whatever régime has engulfed them. This may well mean that he must come to terms with that régime, whatever it may be. For if he cannot do his work if he is in exile, he will be equally unlikely to be able to perform it if he is in prison or dead. Nor is it likely to be done if the Church of which he is a minister is the object of systematic attack.

This consideration has been responsible for some of the most painful dilemmas with which men have been confronted in modern times. In fact most men have been agreed on the principle that the Church's pastoral duties must come first and that the issues of the great debate, the legitimacy of a government or the propriety of its methods, must give way to them. Yet if a Church accepts a régime in order that it may do its work, or not separate itself from its people, it may find that it has associated itself with something that defiles it, as was the case with Cardinal Innitzer when he welcomed Hitler to Vienna. Moreover, even when a régime does not openly attack Christianity, or when it proclaims, as most régimes find it convenient to proclaim, the principle of religious freedom, the conditions of life which it imposes may make it impossible for a Christian Church to do what it is its duty to do, or to tolerate what the State is doing. To make things worse, this situation is likely to develop piecemeal, point by point, administrative decision following administrative decision with secular and spiritual issues adroitly and inextricably confused, and the leaders of a Church may be faced with a series of agonizing problems. How long must they be content to do their best with the opportunities left open to them, or when must they make a stand? What matters shall they pass over in silence or upon what matters must they speak out, with all the disastrous results which outspoken rebuke will certainly entail?

Decisions on these problems will not be made easier, and the sequel to such decisions may be made much more disastrous, if there are people in other countries who are rather clamorously eager that the Church should go into opposition either to establish a principle or because it seems to suit the needs of secular politics. Yet this is normally the position. It is in fact rather easy for those from whom many of the ugly complications are hidden to demand an absoluteness of principle which in fact the situation does not permit, particularly when that principle seems to coincide with their own side in the great debate. Indeed, men and women living in security are sometimes, no doubt unconsciously, rather anxious to hear stories of heroic sacrifice; particularly when they help to sustain their indignation against their opponents, secular or ideological. Neither of these attitudes is tolerable. Courage and devotion have in fact been abundantly shown, and to them admiration must be given unstinted, but charity and knowledge are also necessary, and so is caution lest the lot of Christians who cannot be rescued shall be made worse. The tragic results of violent but inoperative European agitation on behalf of Armenian Christians under Turkish rule should be very carefully considered.

Nevertheless the great debate must go on, questions of absolute principle must be raised, and it is clear that the problem of religious persecution is very relevant to them. It would be very dangerous and wrong if we did not consider it.

My subject is religious persecution in certain countries in Europe since 1945, but these limitations have only been settled because the time and space available are themselves limited; for this is only one act in a much larger tragedy. Probably the curtain should be raised in 1917 with the Russian revolution, and even so it would have to be remembered that significant events had taken place before the play started. Certainly the experiences of Christians in Russia, particularly in the ten years that followed the revolution, are clearly relevant, so are the experiences of Christians and Jews under the Nazis in Germany; so too are the horrible things which were done during the Spanish civil war, or during the period of communist violence in Greece; and so too is the fate of Christians, Orthodox or Lutheran or Roman Catholic, in Latvia, Lithuania and Esthonia, of whom no news is bad news.

Some of this was no doubt simply the natural result of a period of civil violence; but very much of it seems to point to the same issues, the issues raised by the attack of the modern totalitarian State, or the passions which seek to make it totalitarian—be they fascist or communist or nationalist—on any organization or body of belief which might be hostile, or which cannot easily conform to a desired pattern, or may simply provide a convenient target for hatred. The object of attack may be a Christian Church, or Christian beliefs, but it need not be so; the Jews have been in all probability the worst sufferers, scientists have been eliminated who would not conform to a state-imposed orthodoxy, and the hand of persecution has been very heavy on all manner of political dissidents from the extreme right to the extreme left. For the primary cause is not a simple hatred of Christianity as a form of belief; it is rather the conception of the State, not as a framework in which people can live their own lives, but as an instrument to carry into effect one living 'monolithic' idea at the expense of everything else.

Normally such an idea is conceived as being what is, or what ought to be, the 'will of the people', and this monolithic, self-consciously ideological conception of the State is a phase, probably in many cases a necessary phase, in the progress of democracy among the peoples of the world; that is, in the transmutation of the State and society from things based on custom and passive complaisance to things based on opinion and active popular assent. But even if it is a phase in the development towards majority rule, it is not one which teaches much respect for minority rights. A newly liberated, newly self-conscious nation will normally require, to quicken itself into life and meaning, a powerful, rather hysterical emotion which will be very jealous of anything which might divide allegiance or act as a rival. It will normally be obtained by the passionate indoctrination of a large number of people, usually young people, without the intellectual experience which would give them any appreciation of anything outside its ambit. Such devotees are not likely to find it easy to understand that a man can reverence other values without seeking to betray those to which they are so fiercely attached, and it is likely that their emotion will be maintained at its appropriate pressure by the stimulus of hatred, the hatred of foreign enemies or of domestic traitors. The spirits which men call to their aid in order to awaken or conquer society are not likely to be merciful or tolerant spirits, and the plan on which they seek to remould society is not likely to have much room for dissidents or exceptions.

These conditions have not been confined to Europe. As European ideas, democracy, nationalism, communism, have spread through Asia, so also have these tendencies. For instance, in 1949 the communists defeated the nationalists in China and overran the country. After a short breathing-space there followed the forcible extrusion of foreign Christian missionaries. Before the communist victory the Roman Catholics seem to have had nearly 6000 missionaries in China—bishops, priests and members of religious orders. These were reduced in due course to ninety-three, four bishops (two of them in prison), one Prefect-Apostolic in prison, sixty-two priests (twenty of whom were in prison), three monks and twenty-six nuns. It is difficult to calculate the exact number of Protestant missionaries, for the records are distributed among a good many different denominations and in a good many different countries. There may have been about 2000 foreign Protestant missionaries, most of whom have been withdrawn or forcibly deported; the China Inland Mission alone has withdrawn 637. It is not apparently easy to discover what has been the fate of the native clergy or laity, Roman Catholic or Protestant; the Roman Catholics believe that of the 2000 or more native priests, 193 have been imprisoned and 127 killed; and there seems little doubt that native Christians of other denominations have been subjected to treatment under which some were killed, some died, and some committed suicide.

For this operation has not been conducted without savagery. On the whole, the foreign Protestant missionaries seem to be agreed that in general they have suffered less in the way of actual imprisonment than might have been expected, and that American missionaries have suffered worse in this matter than the British, probably because Americans were politically more dangerous than the British. I have the names of eighteen Protestant missionaries who have been imprisoned, some for short periods, some for as much as five years. Of these, two died in prison, one apparently under torture, and there have been cases of 'brain washing'. Many others underwent house arrest in conditions under which two at least died. In general the Roman Catholics seem to have suffered more severely than the Protestants, and this, at least in part, for a reason which is relevant elsewhere. The Protestant organization is normally looser than the Roman Catholic, and the Protestants have been able to adopt the policy of withdrawing foreign missionaries and leaving the Church in the hands of native autonomous organizations to whom the presence of a foreigner would be an embarrassment. This the Roman Catholic Church cannot so easily do, and even if foreign Roman Catholic ecclesiastics are withdrawn, the disciplined subordination of their Church to Rome remains a religious necessity. At some point the Roman Catholic Church in China must be subject to the control of a foreign centre in Europe which is unavoidably suspect.

It cannot be claimed that this account is complete or wholly correct, but from all accounts one significant consideration seems to stand out. The ostensible, and probably the real, motive behind these expulsions and persecutions has been political rather than religious. Christians have been attacked not so much because they maintained an objectionable form of belief as because it was thought that Christian organizations might lead to counter-revolutionary activities, or because of their association with foreign and 'imperialist' forces outside China. Normally they have been attacked as foreigners, and other foreigners, merchants and business men, have shared their fate. Where a definite charge has been levelled at a particular individual it has been a strictly political charge, a charge of sabotage or of spying.

In fact many of these accusations seem to have been obviously either trivial or factitious; trivial as in the case of the matron of a hospital who was charged with 're-actionary activities', tried and deported because she objected to probationer nurses leaving the patients un-attended in order to join in patriotic rallies; or factitious as in several notorious cases where the authorities have tried to substantiate very unlikely accusations of spying by putting savage pressure on the accused person or on potential witnesses. But the nature of these charges prob-ably shows what was foremost in the minds of those who made them, or of the public to which they wished to appeal; and where Christianity has been freed from foreign influence or political suspicion it seems to have been tolerated; certainly native Christians have been per-mitted to make broadcasts and issue manifestos in favour of a Christianity which they claimed had been purified from the corrupting taint of Western imperialism and capitalism.

All this fits into the modern pattern. In previous epochs much of the thought of mankind was directed towards values which were held to be eternal. Con-sequently a man might be persecuted for what he believed, or might lead others to believe, on such matters lest souls should go to hell. Of course in the motive for such persecutions considerations of secular policy were not always absent, and a great deal of ordinary natural ferocity masqueraded as religious ardour. But the ostensible motive was religious. Nowadays men are more concerned with what they hope will happen on this earth. They may claim to be indifferent as to what men affect to believe about God or eternity; they may in fact be indifferent, but that will not prevent them from persecuting men and women on account of their religion. If the religious motive is absent, then the secular motive will predominate; if what is inspired by the religious motive does not subordinate itself to secular necessity, then men and women will be punished, not on account of their religious opinions, but on account of actions or omissions in secular matters which it is believed that their religious connexions and predilections make probable. The difference between this and the old-style religious persecution may not be very great; a charge of treason and a charge of heresy may lead to the same sentence. The situation may be confused by the fact that particular religious organizations may in fact have become involved in secular politics; but all historical experience suggests that, unless men are careful and critical, the suspicion of political nonconformity always outruns any realistic calculation of political danger. In a new materialistic revolutionary state men are not likely to be careful and critical in their evaluation of the political danger or inconvenience of the actions or associations of religious people, whose beliefs will in any case seem to them to be absurd. Therefore, whether the Church is a real political opponent, or whether it is not, it will still be in danger.

This situation can be seen, dimly perhaps because the situation is unfamiliar and the facts obscure, but none the less convincingly, in China. The driving force behind the communist revolution would seem to be nationalism, nationalism expressed in communist categories but none the less nationalism, the determination that China should remake herself for herself by exorcizing the influence of such powers as Great Britain and the United States, which, it is held, have in the past enslaved and exploited her. There is certainly no need to accept the communist version of the history of China's relations with those countries, or to admit into one's vocabulary without analysis those equivocal terms of abuse, 'colonialism', 'imperialism' and 'exploit'; but, taking into account all that has happened in the last 150 years, it must probably be agreed that this desire on the part of the Chinese communists is not unnatural nor wholly indefensible.

Yet the sequel seems to show to what extremes such a natural secular passion will lead. It would be difficult to believe, if the matter were to be fairly considered, that many of the missionaries who have been driven out of China presented on any rational calculation any threat at all to the integrity or autonomy of China, or to the success of the Chinese revolution. On the contrary, from the most strictly secular point of view, it would seem that the labours of many of them both in education and in medical work were of great use to the people, and that they were devoting their lives without afterthought to the benefit of the Chinese. This was, however, a matter in which rational and humane calculations appear to have had little place. There was no place either for such considerations or for the missionaries in the new China, and their expulsion was facilitated by a system of justice which has as its object, not the punishment of proved wrongdoing or the breaches of a known law, but the elimination of individuals or classes of individuals who are thought to be undesirable. The guilt of such persons being assumed, it only remains for the State to use all the means at its disposal to ensure that they should make appropriate confessions; and the Chinese government seems to have surpassed even other communist governments in the merciless patience with which it has set itself to extract confessions.

What has happened seems indeed to be one example of the ruthlessness of so much modern political planning, the fierceness and danger of the organized passion which is the motive force of so much modern political power. But probably it would be best to consider these matters in countries which, though remote and unfamiliar, are less remote than China, and to turn to consider the situation in those countries in Europe which were overrun by communists in 1945.

There are eight territories in question, Poland, East Prussia, Hungary, Czechoslovakia, Bulgaria, Rumania, Yugoslavia and Albania. They belong to the troubled side of Europe, where the forces of history have left results which are peculiarly harsh and confusing. In the turmoil of the past, nation has been thrown violently up against nation, and then they have been left to live alongside one another in circumstances which perpetuated the memories of ancient hatreds and ancient wrongs. Secular dominion has very often extended over national boundaries and has been naturally hated as alien, and often rightly resented as oppressive. Often enough Christian

Churches also have become involved in these rivalries, and have become the symbols of secular domination or national rivalry. So the seeds of bitterness were sown here before 1945.

Three of these territories, Poland, Czechoslovakia and Hungary, are predominantly Roman Catholic; three, Rumania, Bulgaria and Yugoslavia, are Orthodox, and one, East Prussia, holds a large Protestant population. There were also large groups of Uniats, that is, people with Orthodox rites but accepting the Roman obedience, in Galicia (which was Polish before 1939) and in Rumania. In Croatia in the north of Yugoslavia there is a Roman Catholic population. There are also Protestants in Hungary, Bulgaria and elsewhere, and Orthodox in countries that are predominantly Roman Catholic. In Albania there are Orthodox and Roman Catholics, but the majority of the people are Moslem.

After 1945 these countries passed under communist control, and all except one, Yugoslavia, are ruled by governments dominated by Russia. Communist control meant the complete reconstruction of the institutions of these countries, the dispossession of the land-owning and capitalist classes, the break-up of the great estates, the revolutionizing of the political system, the liquidation of existing political parties and the installation of puppet dictatorial governments. It also meant the triumphs of a cause which is, as a matter of theory, explicitly hostile to Christianity. For communists Christianity is an outworn superstition, finally exploded by what they crudely suppose to be science; it is also for them a system which the possessing classes used, in earlier stages of society, to

37

consecrate their title-deeds and to keep the working classes in subjection; and whatever the tactical necessities of the moment, the ultimate object must be to eliminate it. However, what has happened since 1945 has not, clearly, been done under the impulse of communist afflatus alone, for one of the results of the change has been the forcible reconversion of the Uniats in Galicia and Rumania to the Orthodox Church.

The course of the trouble that has developed between Church and State in these countries can perhaps to some extent be plotted by marking the blows struck at various prominent Church leaders in them. In October 1946 the Cardinal Archbishop Stepinać, the Roman Catholic Archbishop in Croatia, was sentenced to imprisonment for sixteen years on a charge of complicity in outrages committed by Roman Catholic Croats on Orthodox Serbs during the war. In 1948 five important members of the Roman Catholic Church in Albania were executed. In November 1948 Bishop Ordass, the senior Lutheran Bishop in Budapest, was sentenced to two years' imprisonment after conviction for currency offences, but really because he opposed the government's educational policy. In February 1949 Cardinal Mindszenty in Hungary was tried on a charge which was tantamount to treason and sentenced to imprisonment for life; in the same month fifteen Protestant pastors in Bulgaria were convicted of espionage and currency offences, after a trial against which the British government protested. In 1951 the Roman Catholic Archbishop Beran in Prague in Czechoslovakia, already under house arrest, was taken to some unknown place without trial. In September 1953

Cardinal Wyszynsky, the Roman Catholic Primate of Poland, suffered the same fate.

These are of course only the most eminent of the victims. Other churchmen have been tried and imprisoned, or imprisoned without trial. At one time it is said that as many as 600 Roman Catholic Uniat priests in Rumania were in prison. It would be difficult to say in any case how many of the faithful laity have suffered, or what they have suffered. For in such countries as these the terms of life, employment or starvation, liberty or imprisonment, or exile from which return is unlikely, are very much more at the discretion of the government than we can easily recognize; while spies and informers penetrate everywhere.

As in China, where there has been a trial the charge has been political. Of course as in China the offence charged in court may have little relation to the real reason for attack. It cannot be emphasized too strongly that, unless a State possesses a satisfactory system of justice, there is little reason to believe that there is much connexion between the offences of which a political prisoner has been convicted and anything he may have done, or the reason for which the government wishes to punish him. The most notorious case is that of Cardinal Mindszenty. He was charged with offences which amounted to treason, and he signed a confession. The form and appearance of the document has excited the deepest suspicion, but the kind of treatment that produced it is matter more for certainty than suspicion. It is not, I think, a question of drugs. Drugs certainly exist which remove a man's control of his words and thoughts under examination, such as the extremely ill-named 'truth' drug, which has been used in the United States. However, there seems to be no evidence that drugs were used in this case, and in fact they are not necessary.

The necessary technique has now been described often enough and with sufficient authenticity to be perfectly well known. It is the technique of continuous interrogation, with denial of sleep to the prisoner, who is given the minimum of food and drink. It is extremely effective; very few people are able to hold out against it, and in most cases it reduces the human mind to more or less complete subservience to the wishes of its captors. Indeed it is important in the interests of humanity to establish the fact that, where there is a suspicion that it has been used, any subsequent confession by the victim is quite worthless as evidence, and will only be accepted as having any relation to truth by the criminally interested or the criminally gullible. This technique has very often been used in communist countries to prepare a political prisoner for trial, and some such method was probably used in this case. Indeed, so notorious did the circumstances of communist trials become that the subsequent removal and imprisonment without trial of Archbishop Beran and Cardinal Wyszynsky may have come to seem to be a more excellent way.

Nevertheless, as in China, the political pretext for the attack is significant. The modern State normally claims that it does not punish men for what they think but only for what they do, or perhaps are likely to do. In all these States I believe freedom of belief is supposed to be officially guaranteed; and nowadays where secular statesmen become involved in a conflict with the clergy it is common form for them to declare that they are not concerned with men's private beliefs, but that action has had to be taken against politically minded clergymen who have gone out of their sphere and intruded into secular politics. It is important to realize that in a sense this may be true. Even the most austerely conceived secular policy on the part of a statesman who has no wish to touch religious belief may interfere with actions and conditions which those beliefs necessarily imply, and this is more likely to happen if the policy-makers chance to believe that the Christian religion is an exploded and obnoxious superstition. If this happens, it will be the duty of religious leaders to resist the secular policy of the government in order to try to secure that they shall be able to fulfil their most purely spiritual duties. Thus they will be involved in secular politics, the more seriously if they live in a State which does not tolerate opposition. The specific charges against Cardinal Mindszenty can be neglected, but it might easily be argued that he had interfered rather violently in secular politics. He had been a pertinacious, even a clumsy and arrogant, opponent of the communist government; after all, he was a very courageous, forthright man of peasant stock, accustomed to saying what he thought was right without considering the consequences. The important point is that the actions of the State were of such a nature that it would have been difficult even for a more dexterous man in his position not to oppose the secular policy of the government without betraying the purely spiritual needs of his flock.

The lesson to be learnt from the present situation is,

I think, this. No guarantee of freedom of belief, or of any other form of freedom, is worth anything when it is given by men who accept no philosophy of freedom and do not respect any of the values which such a philosophy teaches. Nor can freedom in spiritual matters and freedom in secular matters be separated, so that the one is enjoyed while the other is denied. Where there is a belief in freedom and the reality of secular freedom, a religious body can continue in security even if the views it entertains are obnoxious to the government. Elsewhere it will never be secure, for it is always possible for the State, particularly the socialist or communist State, without openly denying to men the freedom to entertain any beliefs that they desire to entertain, and without openly interfering with religious practices, to impose such a pattern on society as to make the independent life of the Church an impossibility. When the leaders of the Church attempt to struggle against the imposition of such a pattern they are naturally thrown into opposition to the government, and that in a single-party State is apt to be considered to be sedition. Where the courts of law are the mere instruments of government policy, this charge can be substantiated by convicting them of appropriate offences, and they can be exhibited to the world as if their primary interest was political reaction and not the spiritual interests which they purport to serve.

In most of the countries overrun something of the same programme has been observed. In general, religious services have been left free; sometimes they have been interrupted by mobs who have maltreated the priest or the worshippers, and no doubt at times this has been done with the licence or encouragement of the government; no doubt also government agents watch them to see who attends them; but in general they are left undisturbed. Visitors to communist countries often mark the fact that the Churches are well attended as evidence that the practice of religion there is free. Standing by itself, it is not very good evidence.

On the other hand, certain steps are normally taken which drastically alter the position of the Church in the community. The first is in the circumstances natural and not unreasonable; it is the separation of Church and State where these have been united. That is followed by a large expropriation of Church property. This too is a natural part of a larger policy not directed specifically at the Church. Yet it may hit a Church hard, for it must be difficult in a communist country for the clergy to subsist even on the simplest terms on what the faithful can afford them out of their daily stock; and the alternative is to accept payment by the State, which places them in a very dangerous position. At the same time, most of the institutions which the Church has built up, hospitals, orphanages, charitable endowments of various sorts, seminaries and places of education are confiscated.

Many of these institutions remain in the hands of the State, as representing activities which the State alone may organize and control. But sometimes they are placed in the hands of subservient clergy, for there is normally an attempt to develop a religious movement which will be docile to the State and useful for the purposes of propaganda. It is normally possible to find priests for this purpose who are confused, or complacent, or ambitious;

and if the ecclesiastical authorities try to subject such men to normal ecclesiastical discipline, they may get into trouble. However, all the ordinary working of the ecclesiastical machine may be seriously impeded. Key men are arrested on various charges, movement may be difficult, communications abroad impossible; and apart from anything else it will not be easy for the rulers of the Church to make their views known. Indeed all printing and publication is likely to come under the control of the government, and it may be very difficult to give general circulation to any printed declaration, newspaper or book which expresses the point of view of the Church. On the other hand, the rulers of the Church may be pressed to make statements which will serve the purposes of the government, but which perhaps they do not believe to be true.

However, the most bitter trouble is likely to come over the control of the organizations which influence the minds of young people and children. After all, to secure the control of the minds of the young is to secure control of the future, complete control if the control of the young can be complete and maintained in its completeness. If it could be sure that future generations were and would remain in proper custody, a totalitarian State could almost afford to abandon the existing generation of adults and elderly people as incorrigible. Consequently the youth organizations and youth movements within any Church come very soon to be the object of concentrated attack, while the schools are secularized and their teaching brought under strict government supervision.

Now even in a liberal State the problem of what shall be taught in government schools very often presents a difficult dilemma. On the one hand, the schools are provided by the community for the community, and therefore it may seem that the community should control what is taught in them; on the other hand, the parents of particular children probably have a natural right, certainly a natural desire, that their children should be brought up in the beliefs which they themselves hold. With goodwill, and a real desire to recognize the rights of particular individuals and particular denominations, it is not always easy to find a satisfactory solution. But in a liberal State which recognizes the rights of private property and private corporations, there will be a safety-valve, for privately endowed and privately supported schools, or partially privately endowed and partially privately supported schools may supply education to the children of those whose beliefs are not those of the majority. In a communist State this safety-valve is likely to be absent, independent places of education are likely to be harried, non-communist teachers in university and school to be dismissed; and there will be little conception of individual right and no goodwill. Religious teaching may be permitted for such as desire it, but what will be normally taught in the schools will be dogmatic communist doctrine, and attempts are likely to be made to turn children against their parents and to victimize those who remain faithful to them. There is no more cruel weapon, no pain is more poignant, than when parents are attacked through their children; that is like what Henry James called in his ghost story 'the turn of the screw'.

The situation can be studied in the different histories of these separate countries. Indeed it ought to be studied, in order to see how possible it is to produce a situation in which it is very difficult for a Christian Church to serve God as a free institution, after the manner in which it believes it was intended to serve God. This is likely to produce trouble between the rulers of the State and the leaders of the Church. The issues between them may seem to be issues of secular politics; they will, however, be spiritual issues. But they will not derive from the general issues of the great debate, the problem whether the State is properly constituted or no, still less from the general diplomatic warfare which divides the world.

This challenge has been met with great courage. The public statements of some of the Roman Catholic prelates involved have been singularly noble documents, dignified, restrained but outspoken, made by men who knew perfectly well what might happen to them. What they have claimed would seem to be basic human freedoms; but there has been a difference of behaviour between the various Christian Churches. On the whole the Protestant and Orthodox Churches have found it easier to come to terms with communist governments than have the Roman Catholics.

As in China, this is in part due to a difference in organization. The Protestant organization is normally looser, and less massive, than the Roman Catholic organization; and both the Protestant and Orthodox Churches are likely to be more nearly autonomous in the particular countries in which they exist, while the Roman Catholic Church must by its theory remain under the control of an extra-national head. Free communication with Rome must be maintained if the Church is to be for

Roman Catholics what it ought to be, and obviously this lays them open to suspicion and attack, particularly since their head is in the suspect West and is clearly in close alliance with forces in Italy, in Spain, in the United States and in other countries which are in active conflict with communism; a suspicion which has no doubt been deepened by the fact that in July of 1949 it was thought necessary to promulgate in Rome an open condemnation of communism. Yet, as a matter of fact, there seems to be no reasonable ground for a belief that the papacy has allowed its power to be used for diplomatic purposes by other countries against the communists, or that it was organizing an anti-communist war, or that the organization of the Roman Catholic Church was being used for the subversion of the existing régimes; not even in Poland, a predominantly Roman Catholic country upon which a communist régime was imposed by fraud and force of arms, after one of the blackest pieces of treachery in history. In fact, the conditions which have been imposed by the State upon the work of the Roman Catholic Church in Poland would seem to be amply sufficient to account for any trouble there has been between the ecclesiastical and secular authorities. Yet, however unjust, it must probably be allowed that the suspicion of Rome is natural if all things are taken into account, particularly since communists are committed to a belief in a continuous, unceasing world conflict and are not likely to interpret any evidence as we are likely to interpret it.

However, this difference in the behaviour of the Churches raises profounder and much more difficult problems than is suggested by a mere difference in organization. There are, for instance, probable differences in the historic approach of the various denominations to the problem of the proper relations of Church and State, which make things easier for Protestant and Orthodox Churches under communism than for Roman Catholics. To the Roman Catholic, the Church, with its closely disciplined world-wide organization, must stand aloof and august, in its own field independent of the secular State, steadfastly claiming its rights, one of which is the right to condemn the State for spiritual reasons should need arise. To many Protestants the Church ought to have a more absolutely spiritual existence, less concerned with the things of this world, more certainly free from the trammels of secular policy or even the ownership of property. Such a view makes it easier for some Protestants to accept, or even to approve of, the conditions of society in a communist state; while the Orthodox theory is coloured by historical experience which is essentially different from that of any Western religious body.

For the Orthodox Church has in the past been both at times more closely united with, and at times more widely divided from, the various secular governments under which it has lived than has been the normal experience of most Christian bodies in the West. In the Christian Byzantine Empire in the East the union of Church and State was very close and of a nature not easy to understand in terms of the categories of an ecclesiastical organization which developed in the West, further from the Emperor's shadow, in greater independence. That union was reproduced in Russia and lasted there in one way or another up to the revolution of 1917. On the other hand, from very early on large masses of Orthodox Christians lived under rulers who were not Christians at all, and who would certainly strike hard if there was any suggestion that the real allegiance of their Christian subjects was directed to Christian powers outside their borders. The Christians who lived in the sixth century within the Persian Empire had to face this situation. It became more general with the first conquests of Islam and was continued and extended under the Turks. This situation was reproduced in severer form in Russia after the communist revolution.

And the theory which these conditions have suggested seems to be something on these lines. It is the duty of the Church to accept necessities and to co-operate with whatever secular government it has to live under if that is morally possible. Any normal government represents the principle of order, and therefore it is the duty of members of the Church to submit to it, if they can, for conscience' sake, a view they share with St Paul; possibly also the instinct derived from their remote past makes them more anxious to identify themselves with the secular government of their nation than might be the case with a Western Church. In any case it is the Church's primary task to perform its spiritual functions, to serve the faithful and to maintain the faith; they have learnt from experience that if they are in violent conflict with the secular authorities they will not be free to do this. It is probably in fulfilment of these principles that the metropolitan Sergius in Russia came to some sort of terms with the communist government in the years 1926–7, an alliance which became closer after the Church had rallied to that government at the time of its great peril in 1941 and 1942. Such principles and instincts have also enabled the Orthodox Church to make terms with communist governments elsewhere.

To those of us who live in the West there is likely to be something very displeasing about this. That any Christian Church should make terms with any communist government spoils the symmetry of the great debate. Moreover, we are used to Churches and Christian leaders pronouncing judgment on secular governments and politicians with impunity. We may well believe that this is their primary duty, and that if they are not acting as judges on secular society they are failing in their task. We ought to remember, however, that in Western Europe and the United States we have been the spoilt children of Christendom. In Western Europe and the United States, Christians have normally lived under governments which have either been Christian or liberal; they might attend to spiritual admonition, or if they objected to it or resisted it they might not hit so hard. Nor has there been so necessary a preoccupation with the primary task of keeping the Church in existence. There have been exceptions to this, particularly in the two centuries of mutual persecution that followed the Reformation. But even then the situation was made different by the intricacy of the system of European sovereign States who variously sheltered a variety of religious denominations. In the east of Europe the experience has been different and generally harsher.

Yet it is, I suppose, natural to suspect that any collaboration between Christians and communists means that there has been a failure of courage or a surrender of faith. It is hard to be sure that such suspicions are fair. It is not fair to assume a surrender of faith unless there is evidence for it, and in fact the evidence seems to suggest that the Orthodox Church in Russia has done a very remarkable thing in keeping the faith alive in the face of a perfectly ruthless government which wished to destroy it. It has not done this without suffering. Nor can a failure of courage be assumed from immunity from attack. For instance, in 1953 hostile forces seemed to be gathering for an attack on the Protestant Church in East Prussia, the immediate objective being, as so often, the youth movement. The Church prepared itself for persecution. The young people in large numbers expressed their loyalty to the Church, and the authorities of the Church issued a very courageous declaration of principle. The blow never fell. No doubt the reason why the courage of the East Germans was successful sprang from the fact that the Russians did not want large-scale trouble at that particular spot, at that particular moment. But this immunity was not purchased by a surrender of principle on the part of the East Germans.

Indeed, any general moral judgment as to what ought to have been the attitude of Christian Churches towards the communist governments under which they live would be wrong; particularly when it is passed by men who are remote from the spot, ignorant of many of the conditions and of the ecclesiastical traditions of those involved, and yet are interested in the matter. But it is not to be denied that some peculiarly dark dangers arise in this matter of collaboration.

Christians have had at times other reasons for accepting a communist government than the fact that they had to accept an unwanted but unavoidable necessity. A communist government may be harsh and atheistic, it may lack all the institutions which we believe are necessary to secure the free representation of the people or the rule of law, and yet it may be all that exists for the men of a particular nationality, Christians as well as non-Christians, of their own national government. It will therefore be preferable to the governments of foreign States, however free they may be. This will be even more likely to be the case if those governments represent nations they believe they have reason to hate or suspect; nor will they feel the lack of liberal institutions so much if they never fully possessed them. More than this, it is possible that perfectly sincere Christians will nevertheless be attracted by the social objects of communism. There are indeed probably some Balkan countries where the communists have carried through social reforms which were long overdue; and it is natural and indeed right that Christians should be sympathetic with the idea that poverty should be abolished and better social justice should be secured. More than this, again, it is perfectly possible that even Christians should be led to believe that communism stands for peace against war-mongering capitalist and imperialist powers.

This last statement is of course rubbish, and to us palpable rubbish, the clumsy message of a singularly transparent and mendacious propaganda. Alas, we have yet to appreciate the compulsive force of propaganda when it is reiterated daily and there is no other source of knowledge by which it can be checked. Everyone in a communist State is constantly subject to the propaganda of that State, they live with it, they breathe it in, every day and all the time. It alone paints for them the picture of what is going on in the world at large, for they probably have no other source of information, and they are likely to be absolutely ignorant, ignorant to a degree which it is not easy to credit, of facts which may seem to us to be inconsistent with the picture which is being painted for them.

What was probably a remarkable example of that ignorance can be found in the very distressing letter written in 1948 by the Patriarch Alexius in Moscow to the Greek Orthodox Archbishop of Athens Damaskinos. In that letter Alexius protested against the severity of the measures which the Greek government was taking against the communists. Now in actual fact Greece had been the victim in the winter of 1944–5 of a treacherous and brutal attempt by the local communists to seize power by force of arms. In that attack the communists were guilty of savage excesses against the unarmed civilian population. It is calculated that between 12 October 1944 and the end of May 1946, 56,735 unarmed civilians were killed by the communists, many of them in mass murders or individual executions. This included 239 school teachers, 120 doctors and also 275 orthodox priests, who were executed by the communists. In addition to this, 46,871 unarmed civilians were taken as hostages, approximately 28,000 children kidnapped and carried behind the iron curtain, 13,698 old people of both sexes were carried off into communist countries to be put to forced labour. These were terrible blows for a small and poor country which had already suffered the ravages of war, the miseries of occupation and of starvation. In this crisis Archbishop Damaskinos had put himself at the head of his people, he had led them through their time of trouble with the intention of yielding power in the end to a régime chosen by a free vote, which he did. Yet it was to him that the Patriarch Alexius wrote to protest against the infinitely milder measures taken by that government against the communists, measures which by any calculation seem to have been necessary to save Greece from further torment. It is as well to reflect upon the extreme courtesy and moderation of the answer of Damaskinos, in which he treated the protest as the result of misinformation, as no doubt it was.

Such public statements on the part of Christian leaders in communist countries are often distressing enough, particularly when, as is normal, they have obviously been prompted by communist governments to suit their secular ends. The ignorance and misconception they reveal is very dangerous, particularly when one considers that it affects almost everyone living under that particular régime. But far more dangerous are the passions of nationalism. I have said that the ideas which control humanity take to themselves flesh and blood from the common experiences, the memories bitter or inspiring, the instinctive hopes and hatred, of various groups of men. A normal expression of those common ideas is through the instinctive common feelings and explicit traditions of a nation or people. A universal idea will often, must often, make use of the passions of nationalism, and in turn it will be infected by them. That has been true from time to time of communism in different parts of the world; it is also often true of Christianity or at least of some particular version of Christianity.

In the east of Europe the prevalent form of Christianity is often more closely and intimately connected with the whole life of a people than is normal in the more peaceful societies of the West, where a richer and more varied national secular life has been possible. Under Turkish rule, for instance, the Christian peasant found in his Church not only his religion but most of what was left to him of his national life. Except for old ballads and memories, his nation was gone, he lived under alien rule; but his priest remained. Consequently the nature of a man's religious obedience, Roman Catholic or Orthodox, came to be closely bound up with his nationality, national boundaries were apt also to become ecclesiastical boundaries, and the interests of particular Churches to be identified with the policies of particular governments. This was not unnatural—it has happened elsewhere; there is in fact a close analogy in Ireland; but in the present crisis it has had terrible results. The forcible re-conversion of Roman Catholic Uniats in Galicia has been justified because it was held to be an answer to the persecutions inflicted by the Roman Catholic Poles on the Orthodox when they controlled the territory between the wars. In Rumania, the Orthodox Patriarch Justinian has welcomed the forcible re-conversion of the Uniats, because he held that they had been in the past severed from his Church by the oppressions of the Roman Catholic Hapsburgs; but the most difficult and controversial case of a Christian leader caught up in the vortex of nationalist passions is that of the Cardinal Archbishop Stepinać in Croatia.

Croatia is the territory which lies to the north of Bosnia in Yugoslavia. At one time the Croats had been subjects of the Hapsburgs and they are mostly Roman Catholics; but they are also Slavs, and after 1918 Croatia came to form part of the kingdom of Yugoslavia. In that kingdom there was continual trouble between the Croats and the Serbs, and since the Serbs were Orthodox, a symbol for these difficulties was often enough to be found in the difference between the Roman Catholic and Orthodox Churches. In 1941 Yugoslavia was overrun by the Germans and Italians, a puppet Croat régime was set up, and savage outrages were inflicted on the Serbs largely by marauding Croat bands called the Ustashi. There is no doubt about these outrages, which unfortunately included forcible and brutal conversions to Roman Catholicism, and it seems clear that Roman Catholic priests were involved. It was for complicity with these outrages that Archbishop Stepinać was tried and convicted, and though at that time the hand of the communist government of Marshal Tito was also heavy on the Orthodox Serbs many of them felt that Archbishop Stepinać had only received his deserts.

Now the Archbishop had come out with courage and clarity against the communist government and the very savage reprisals that had been inflicted on Roman Catholic priests, and it might be reasonably argued that that was the real reason for his prosecution, and not what might have happened during the war. In addition to this the government may have feared that he represented Italian influences. He himself vigorously denied any responsibility for the outrages of the Ustashi; he declared that he had condemned their cruelties, and that he had also condemned forced conversions, though he pointed out the difficulty in which he was placed when people begged to be received into the Roman Catholic Church in order to save their lives. There is little doubt that his position was one of terrible difficulty, but if his denials are to be accepted there yet remains something to be answered. The Ustashi and the Croats who were guilty were Roman Catholics; no doubt their outrages were the result of savage national feelings, but they committed them in the name of Roman Catholicism. Yet they were not excommunicated either by him or by Rome. When it was a question of opposition to Marshal Tito and the communists, Archbishop Stepinać published his views in a document of great dignity and courage; during the war there was no such public condemnation of the other side in spite of the fact that those guilty were members of his Church.

The point can be put by quoting part of the letter of an Orthodox priest who admired Archbishop Stepinać for his stand against the communists and who himself had suffered imprisonment at the hands of the government of Marshal Tito. He says: 'The comparison of these more or less private letters against the crimes of the Ustashi during the war with the pastoral letter against Tito after it shows quite clearly that Cardinal Stepinać believed there was a great difference between them. In the first case he was acting just as a Christian diplomat; in the second he preferred to be a martyr. His wonderful character allows no doubt of his sincerity in both cases. It means that he did not regard the murder by Roman Catholics of the bodies and souls of thousands of Orthodox Christians in the same light as he did the similar treatment of the Roman Catholics themselves.'

Now the critical facts of this case are bitterly contro-verted by one side or the other, and it would be wrong for me to pass judgment on them or, heaven help us, on a man who has stood with courage for his view of the truth. Yet, however interpreted, they draw attention to one very serious factor. Europe is filled with very strong political feelings. There are not only the ordinary violent hopes and fears inherent in a dangerous and difficult political situation; but in the east of Europe, and not only in the east of Europe, there are memories more vivid and disturbing than anything we in England know. In the east of Europe men look back on a past which has been consistently harsher than our own. Life has been harder, violence greater and governments rougher than anything that we have had to face for many centuries. In these circumstances personal conduct has often been heroic, and in all communions Christians have often enough had to show an absoluteness of devotion and sacrifice for their faith which is not so often demanded by the circum-stances of a more peaceful and humdrum existence. On the other hand, the violences of secular life have often tended to slip into religion, particularly where the life, the very existence of a nation was bound up with the life of its Church, Roman Catholic or Orthodox. Fierce secular feelings may cause religious persecution, and be condoned by religious leaders. The way in which such feelings play with Christianity can be seen in the forces around the unhappy Cardinal Archbishop Stepinać; whether, or how far, they diverted him from his duty as a Christian priest and reduced him to be 'just a Christian diplomat' must be left for others to decide; the important fact is that in this case they can be seen at work. I certainly believe that they are also present in some of the statements of the Patriarch Justinian about the reconversion of the Uniats in Rumania.

There is no occasion for self-righteousness here. If we have not faced these rigours we are not, I think, entitled to sit in judgment on their results. Moreover, this particular difficulty, which is so easily recognizable in the strong harsh colours of the life of the Balkans, is one that in much subtler forms we all have to face in our own way; and it is particularly relevant to the appeal to Christianity by men engaged in the great debate. It is very hard indeed to decide how far one's views on Christianity are in fact coloured by the terms of one's life, or to be at all sure that secular prejudices, affections and dislikes have not in fact mixed themselves with what present themselves to the mind as purely spiritual convictions. This danger is certainly always present when Christians as Christians take part in politics. Clearly in many problems of secular politics spiritual issues of great importance are involved, upon which Christians as Christians ought not to be silent. Yet to make declarations on secular politics, to support one line of action and resist another, normally entails association with secular allies, whose motives may not all the time be wholly inspired by a pure zeal for Christianity. Indeed, they may be anxious to use the Christian name to secure objects which have little to do with Christianity and might perhaps be repugnant to it. Moreover, in all political controversy there is apt to be misrepresentation of other men's motives and an appeal to hatred or at least to dislike; it is not easy for any contestant to avoid these things, yet it is by no means well when they slip into pronouncements which claim to express the pure principles of the religion of Christ. No doubt it is necessary to incur these dangers when the alternative is to keep silence on matters on which there is a duty not to keep silence; but it is also necessary to recognize their existence.

There is in fact one consideration which is immediately relevant. We may well say that those Churches and religious bodies that have made their peace with communism have entered into a very perilous collaboration. They are in danger of being exploited by ruthless forces for secular and possibly evil ends. They may find it necessary to assent to conditions which they ought to refuse, to be blind to facts which they ought to condemn, or at the least to make distressing pronouncements when they are in unhappy ignorance of the facts. These things are no doubt true, but are they not also true of the Christian Churches who collaborate with the other side? Are they not also entering into a perilous collaboration? Is there not some danger that Christianity shall be rather anxiously enlisted to defend the comforts, the wealth, even the inequalities and injustices of bourgeois society? May there not be a danger that Christians so engaged may be conveniently silent, or make pronouncements on matters on which their knowledge is neither complete nor just?

None of this, however, should lead us to condone or deny what Christians have suffered under communism. It is wrong not to call things evil when they are evil, or to overlook or condone oppression or persecution when men have undoubtedly been persecuted and oppressed. Indeed, it is necessary to go further. It is necessary to mark the fact that in a properly working liberal society many of these oppressions could not have occurred. With a proper system of law Cardinal Mindszenty would never have been condemned and Cardinal Wyszynsky and Archbishop Beran, and many others, would never have been imprisoned. Under liberal governments there would have been no forcible re-conversion of the Uniats. Church institutions and property would have been secure, Church members not subject to the attentions of the secret police or to adverse discrimination in civil life; Church publications would be free, Church administration not interfered with. Youth movements would not have been attacked, and though it cannot be said that in all liberal States a satisfactory solution to the problem of State education has been reached, yet the situation is normally infinitely more satisfactory for Christian parents under a liberal régime than it is in a communist State.

In fact there is no doubt that it is much easier for a Christian Church to exist and do what it has to do in a liberal State, even if that State is agnostic, or perhaps atheist, than under a hostile totalitarian government. But what does this mean? Does it mean that Christianity endorses the principles of the liberal State, or simply that it accepts them only when they are the best terms it can get? Ought a Christian Church to work, not for a liberal

State, but for a Christian totalitarian State which shall enforce its own brand of Christianity? A good many contingent questions spring from this main one. Have all organized bodies a right to a free existence within a Christian State, or only Christian Churches or a particular Christian Church? Has all opinion a right to freedom of utterance or only such opinions as favour Christianity? Have all parents a natural right to control the education of their children, or only Christian parents belonging to a particular denomination? And so on and so forth; but they are all comprehended in the one large question, is the liberty which we demand only for Christians because they are Christians, or do we demand it for men because they are men?

These questions are not in truth relevant to the problems of the men and nations which I have been trying to discuss. Here men and women are faced with more elementary questions, whether the faith shall survive, whether the Church shall be free to continue to do what it has to do; it would be impertinent to raise in relation to them the problem of what might happen in quite different circumstances, or even of what they themselves might do in quite different circumstances. The main problems here are not those raised by the general application of some universal theory of liberty. They are rather raised by the actions of States whose rulers hold no belief in liberty unless it be realized in the terms of their own dogma and through the results of their endeavours. The issue here is concerned with the power and pride of the all-sufficient, all-intrusive secular State, having behind it the impact of those forces, part opinion part passion, which play so great a role in the modern world. These creeds are not necessarily ignoble; in some cases no doubt they are an inevitable stage in the awakening of a nation's self-consciousness; but they are normally absolute, limited, pitiless, unjust and blind.

Nevertheless, the problem of the relation between secular liberty and Christianity is very relevant to the subjects I wish to discuss, and in my next three chapters I will turn to the connexion between Christianity and the general habits and standards of liberal society, and then to the problem of liberty itself.

CHAPTER III

CHRISTIANITY AND LIBERAL
DEMOCRACY: INTRODUCTORY

IN my first chapter I said that propagandists for the Western liberal democracies often enough enforced their case by talking about societies or governments with 'Christian' traditions as opposed to governments with 'pagan' or 'materialist' principles on the wrong side of the iron curtain. In fact such phrases as these have formed part of the recognized stock-in-trade of publicists and orators of the more solemn sort, who do not always subject themselves to the irksome necessity of saying what precisely it is that they mean. Now I think there is some truth behind these phrases; what it is and how far it goes are problems that we shall have to consider, but first it is necessary to realize that there is considerable danger in their use.

Where the danger lies is obvious; indeed, I have already tried to suggest it. Christianity is a strong name, for many of us the strongest we possess, and there is an obvious temptation to use it as emotional cover behind which to hide things which are less defensible. The temptation is the more dangerous because we are not in the least likely to make use of the crude ideas which have often enough been attributed to Christians in the past. Charles Kingsley and Karl Marx suggested that Christianity was used as an opiate draught for overburdened people; it has been believed that religion was prized because it taught the poor to be content with their lot; it enabled men to pay them very little now by promising them an everlasting reward hereafter, a transaction which would cost the capitalist nothing—or rather he thought that it was going to cost him nothing. No one talks like that nowadays, or (I believe) thinks like that, and I rather doubt whether anyone has ever thought precisely in the simple and cynical terms which have been of such use to satirists. As I see it the temptation comes in subtler form as an unconscious motive behind the perfectly sincere desire to appeal to Christianity in the general defence of the civilization and methods of the Western and liberal States.

The argument which justifies this appeal is, after all, reasonably convincing. In the formation of the traditions of Great Britain and the other liberal States, Christianity has undeniably played a considerable part; they are opposed to States which are explicitly based on a philosophy which repudiates Christianity. On the other side of the iron curtain Christian Churches are persecuted, on our side they are free; our institutions protect Christians in the practice of their religion. Therefore ours is a society based on Christian traditions and theirs is materialist and pagan. Now I am afraid there is a *non sequitur* here; it is true that Christianity has played its part in forming our traditions, but was it a predominant part? And does it predominate now? Or does practical materialism in our case strangle it as effectively as does their theoretical materialism? It may be so, or it may not; the matter is obviously a subject for inquiry. In any case the fact that the Christian Church is free to operate in a particular society does not necessarily mean that it approves of the rules and methods of that society. If Christianity is all that we believe it to be, it may require, for instance, a more commanding position in the State than mere toleration or equality with other opinions would concede to it. It may be so, or it may not; the matter is subject for inquiry.

Here, however, is something which is not subject for inquiry. Without question Western society preserves conditions under which I and others exist very comfortably. It enables me to go to my college chapel without the fact being noted against me by the secret police; it also provides for me comfortable rooms in my college and it enables me to go to dinner in the college hall where I can get food, and wine which is quite often worth drinking. Is there not a fatty residuum here which I am endeavouring to protect by my appeal to Christianity? Nor am I by any means the only man who has a position to lose, comforts to forfeit, if the liberal, non-communist, society which favours us disappears. In invoking Christianity on its behalf, are we not probably unconsciously, at least in part, giving way to a very common human temptation, the temptation to canonize one's own interests? We would be remarkable men indeed if we were altogether free from this taint.

There is also another temptation, the temptation to canonize one's own habits. With short intervals I have lived in Great Britain all my life and I have come to believe that in the British way of life and the peculiar type of freedom which it makes possible there is something of absolute value to all men; I have worshipped with the

Church of England all my life and believe that I have experienced in its services things which are of eternal importance to all men. I am thereby subject to a temptation which is not peculiar either to Englishmen or to Anglicans. What appears to be of absolute value, perhaps the very message of eternity itself, comes to any particular man in a way peculiar to himself—through particular institutions, through particular types of people, by means of particular types of devotion and expression; the temptation is to confuse the medium with the message it conveys, and then to believe that absolute value can only be conveyed by those particular methods and institutions, and then that in those methods and institutions themselves lies absolute and universal value. And this leads to the very common sin of idolatry, the substitution of the particular for the universal, the temporal for the eternal, the creature for the creator.

I think that both of these temptations are present whenever Christianity is invoked in support of a particular way of life. That does not mean, of course, that such invocation is wrong, or at least entirely wrong; but it does mean that we must think very hard before we say that the Christian religion endorses the value of our way of life in its entirety, or endorses our way of life and our institutions and no other. We may be right in our claims, or in some of our claims, but we must be circumspect.

Nevertheless, at first sight, on a rough and ready balance, the judgment here seems not to be difficult. If Western democracy is perhaps not altogether of God, what it has opposed seems to have been, reasonably often, obviously of the devil. I do not want to revive dreadful memories in order to cause hatred, but no good will be served by pretending that things which did happen never happened. I am afraid it is necessary to remember the attempt by the Nazis to destroy the Jews, the extermination chambers at Treblinka and Auschwitz, the conditions of the concentration camps such as Dachau and Belsen, the tortures inflicted by the Gestapo and the state of the slave labour in occupied Europe. Nor should some of the undoubted facts in the Russian record be forgotten: what happened to many independent peasants in the thirties, or to certain subject populations in Central Asia, or to the independent, utterly harmless communities of Lithuania, Esthonia and Latvia; nor may we forget the conditions in the labour camps in the North and in Siberia, nor the tyranny and spying, nor the way in which prisoners have been prepared for trial. Western democracy may not rise very high, and has sometimes fallen disgracefully low, but truly it has never fallen so low as this. Surely so far as its existence has prevented the extension of such things as these, and so far as its principles have forbidden such things as these, to that extent at least it may be called a Christian system.

Here, however, there stands in the road one rather ugly fact. Western democracy as it now exists has developed after Christianity had ceased to be the uniform belief of Western Europe. In those centuries when European countries were at least nominally more uniformly Christian than they are today, things not unlike the deeds we have stigmatized were done in their bounds. They were not perhaps on the massive and horrible scale of the actions of these modern practitioners, but they were done often enough unrebuked and unquestioned, and were sanctioned by long-standing habit, or were part of the routine of respected institutions. For instance, torture formed part of the criminal process, and such cruel punishments as breaking on the wheel formed part of the penal system in many European countries up to, or nearly up to, the French Revolution. In England, in the last two centuries at least, these extreme cruelties in punishment were not often inflicted, and the rights of an accused person were better protected; nevertheless, up to the twenties and thirties of the last century the death sentence was pronounced on minor criminals with an indiscriminate and indecent profusion which was a scandal to Europe, and far too often carried out. Trade in negro slaves was legal for Englishmen till 1808, and negro slavery legal in English dominions till 1834; and in other Christian countries both existed till later than that. And throughout these Christian centuries the lot of the poor was often very miserable and the natural inequality of rich and poor was normally assumed.

These things are bad enough, but there is worse to come. Not only did Christians permit them, they did very terrible things in the name of Christianity itself. They massacred non-Christians, or Christians with whom they disagreed. They imprisoned and tortured non-Christians and Christians with whom they disagreed, they put such men and such women to shameful and painful deaths, and they believed that they did these things in the service of Christ.

We know that they were wrong. It is to be hoped that no one exists today who does not contemplate with horror the idea of racking a religious opponent till he has endured the extremity of pain and then completing the proceedings by piously tearing out his bowels or burning him alive. No one today would accept the arguments in favour of negro slavery which not so long ago pious folk thought that they found in their bibles. Everyone nowadays realizes it is morally wrong that some people should be doomed from the mere accident of birth to live lives of crippling toil, semi-starvation and ignorance. But if we accept these changes we must accept also the reality and moral significance of an idea which some religious teachers seem to dislike, the idea of moral progress. All ages may be equidistant from eternity; they have not been in every country equidistant from the slave pen, the quartering block and the stake; and to deny that fact is to deny something which it is morally very dangerous to deny. Indeed, if we are to accept the moral significance of liberal democracy, we must accept the moral significance of the process which brought it into being.

Of course we can only accept that idea with certain caveats. In accepting the fact of progress we are not celebrating our own virtues: we are using the virtues, the spiritual perceptions, of men and women who are, for the most part, dead. Progress is not to be tested by the mere passage of time, nor is it the result of the mere passage of time. It is not necessarily uniform. If men and women have gained a truer conception of certain spiritual values, they have almost certainly lost sight of others. Moral progress is not the same as mechanical progress or progress in organization; for instance, a society may be better equipped and better, even more humanely, organized than ever before, and yet have lost something of its sense of humanity. Moral progress is not inevitable and its results are never secure. The most terrible lesson of this century is the ease and swiftness with which retrogression can take place. One of the nightmares of the period between 1920 and 1939 was that lived through by liberal Germans who watched boys, neighbours' children whom they had known from babyhood, drawn into the Nazi movement and then saw how quickly they became degraded, how absolutely they lost their standards and became truculent and very cruel.

Nevertheless, the fact of moral progress is not to be questioned, and we owe to it the relative humanity of our institutions, which is both a humiliating and a very hopeful reflection. It is humiliating, for it means that many of the things of which we are proud, or even of the feelings we assume to be innate in ourselves, we do in fact owe to others. If I object to the flogging of women or the exploitation of the labour of little children, I probably owe those feelings to philanthropists who taught humanity that such things were wrong. But the reflection is hopeful because if so much has been done more can be done. It lies within the power of mankind to secure that its institutions shall be more humane and more merciful than they are at present; it lies within the power of any nation to secure an even greater improvement within its own bounds. And in every case there is ample room for improvement.

This acceptance of the fact and value of progress, however, presents to Christians one rather uncomfortable problem. Not all moral progress has been the work of

Christians. Much of it has been the work of those who were not Christians; some of them were explicitly the enemies of Christianity and some of them found that their most obstreperous opponents were those who claimed to speak for Christianity. As a matter of fact, it is not particularly easy to say clearly who was responsible for what. Christians took over and developed the ideas of pagan philosophers; deists and non-Christian agnostics based their philosophy on Christian assumptions; Christians again learnt in their turn from deists and non-Christian agnostics, and none of them have been very anxious to confess their debts. Meanwhile the whole field has been repeatedly picked over by polemical writers only anxious to pull out those plums which suited their particular pudding; with the result that a good many statements made about it have been *a priori* declarations adorned with suitable instances and not historical at all. This must have been so, it has been said, because it is known that either Christians or the opponents of Christianity were the apostles of humanity and freedom and therefore it was so, and here are one or two startling examples to carry conviction. Indeed, a certain number of the statements very confidently made about the history of the freedom of opinion require rather careful historical reconsideration. Nevertheless, the fact stands out, unquestionable, unavoidable and very significant, that much of the moral progress to which we are heirs has been the work of men who have never heard of Christianity, or of men who have rejected it.

Very well, be it so. The answer is obvious. The operations of the spirit of God have not been confined to the

Christian Church—not to the whole body of Christian Churches, and still less to one particular branch of the Christian Church. By their fruits ye shall know them: do men gather grapes of thorns or figs of thistles? Wherever justice, mercy and love have been at work, God has been at work, if we Christians have, to our shame, been idle or recalcitrant. We must recognize our debt and accept the results.

The variety of the beliefs of those who have been responsible for human progress suggests, however, another difficulty of a slightly different nature; there has also been a variety of motive. Not all human progress has been the product of justice, mercy and love. There has been dross with the gold; self-interest, the corporate pride of resurgent nations or the results of that very sensible calculation that if I and my friends do terrible things to our enemies they in their turn will do terrible things to us, if they get the chance, and that humane treatment for the individual is desirable because in the last resort that will lead to more comfortable conditions all round. It is probable that only in very few cases has the motive in fact been purely selfish, and in many cases the cause of self-interest has been advanced in support of altruistic principles which its logic, strictly applied, could not sustain. Self-interest has been an explanation offered by those who disliked the idea of a transcendental source of morality, and in many cases it has been a most improbable explanation. Nor can humanity afford to reject what is offered to it with mixed motives; it would not receive much if it did. However, the trouble about mixed motives is that you can never tell what part of the mixture is going to predominate, and the trouble with enlightened self-interest is that you can never tell what private interest enlightenment is going to disclose. Clearly it is necessary to discriminate. The architects of institutions and customs which Christianity may be called upon to endorse need not have been Christians by name, but among their motives there must have been what we would recognize as the Christian motive, and in their results what we consider to be the Christian principle must be realized. Otherwise we shall get into trouble.

Now of course the basic Christian motive, as far as humanity is concerned, should be love for all men and women simply because they are men and women, and the basic Christian principle is its corollary—the recognition of the absolute and eternal value of every individual man and woman and child as children of God. The first seems almost impossible to achieve, and the second is exceedingly difficult to put into practice; nevertheless, they present useful touchstones for the testing of human traditions and institutions. The more nearly these have embodied that motive or vindicated that principle, the greater their right to endorsement by the authority of the Christian name. In no human institution or tradition will that right be complete, but there are gradations from the ideal which will mark the changes from what deserves partial approval to what must be condemned. Where there has not been love there may have been benevolence, where there has been no benevolence there may have been a sense of justice, which is at least a recognition of the value, and so of the rights, of other men and women. Institutions and traditions which embody something of any of these motives have some right to Christian approval whatever their origins and methods, or however foreign and distasteful to us. But so far as the motive is predominantly that of self-gratification, or when any human beings are simply regarded as things without rights, as so much raw material to be used for ends which do not relate to themselves, the system must be condemned.

By these tests the profit-and-loss account of most countries and most political systems is likely to become exceedingly long and complicated, and human beings are in every case quite incapable of doing the sum. In fact there is no sum; you cannot tot up the virtues and deficiencies of any system of government and hope to reach a credit balance which will enable you to call it a Christian government. Even if such a calculation were ever likely to yield a positive result, and it will never do so, you would then have to take account of the spirit in which these institutions are going to be used, the force and direction at any given time of prevalent public opinion; and that is like the wind that blows, mutable and incalculable. There does not exist in the world, and there never has existed, any government which could be called without blasphemy a Christian government, and there does not exist any nation that could be called without blasphemy a Christian nation; and since political systems about which men argue in the great debate—democracy, aristocracy, dictatorship—are generalizations from secular politics and secular governments, it is impossible to say that this or that system is a Christian system of politics, still less the only possible Christian system of politics.

All that you can ask is whether such a system as liberal democracy implies certain traditions and institutions in which the Christian principle and the Christian motive can find partial expression; and whether, if those traditions and institutions are absent, it is more likely that the Christian principle will be set at naught and the Christian motive, so far as the state is concerned, not effective.

And if this question is asked about the liberal democracies I believe the answer is going to be 'yes'. For one thing, there is this tradition of humanity, the tradition that has developed that human beings, and even animals, ought never to have certain extreme pains and miseries inflicted on them, that the dignity and integrity of human beings should be respected, that their lives should be if possible preserved. No doubt it is far feebler than it ought to be, painfully intermittent, tragically restricted in its view. No doubt also it can be relaxed into loose and rather worthless sentimentalism. But it is a fact. As a matter of sober history it has done much to change our institutions from what they were not so very long ago; and while it prevails it forbids such horrors as were practised under either Stalin or Hitler. But these are still possible where the humane tradition is absent and where the motives which might have invigorated it have been transmuted into a harsh political creed which promises much for the future, but cauterizes all sentiment about what individuals may suffer in the present.

Another older tradition is that which has led to the rule of law, and the institutions which embody the rule of law. This may seem less attractive, for it is more technical, and individual examples of its operation are often exceedingly repellent. It is not easy for the sympathetic observer to discern the working of the divine justice on a dismal morning in a dingy city court where the judge or magistrate is dealing with a procession of sordid unfortunates in whose cases bad luck, incapacity and perverted psychology seem too often to be inextricably mixed, and all must be decided within the terms of the 'artificial wisdom of the law'. Yet, even in these lugubrious proceedings, a principle of great importance is present. Unless things are going very wrong no accused person can be punished until the facts of the case have been proved by some objective process, and then only for actions which are a breach of some known law and are culpable by the tenets of some intelligible system of morality. Of course the methods of proof may be questionable; the law may be bad and the underlying conception of morality inadequate. If such defects exist they ought to be remedied, but even where it is not effectively applied the principle is present; and it is important to remember how many of the rights and privileges of civilized society depend for their security on the existence of this principle. It is important to remember what happens in those countries where 'justice' is considered to be no more than a way of enforcing the policy of the moment and the facts are manipulated to suit the accusation.

Now in each of these examples the same moral concept can be recognized; it is the inherent importance and right of the individual for his own sake. Whatever the needs of the generality, it is wrong to inflict extreme pain on an individual because he is an individual, because it is wrong to inflict extreme pain on any man, woman or child, or even perhaps on any animal. However obnoxious or inconvenient he may be, any man has a right to a fair trial simply because he is a man. There is something absolute here which ought to transcend the needs of the State and the demands of the multitude however passionate. I do not say that it always has done so, or always does so, or always will do so, but I do say that there is some recognition here that it ought to do so. The recognition of this principle may be dim, uncertain, and difficult to fit in with the recognition of the rights of other individuals, but there is every difference between what may happen in a State where there is some recognition of this principle and what may happen in a State where there is none.

The same principle is reflected in another tradition which has done much to form liberal institutions, and which is older than democracy. The tradition is that a man ought to be consulted about the decisions which are going to affect him. Of course the application of this principle has often been extremely partial and unreal: it is reasonably unreal in the Britain of today. The chain is very long and loose which stretches between the civil servant in Whitehall who frames the regulation which has to be obeyed, through a House of Commons which passes a very technical bill it has not had time to discuss, to the voter who some years before struggled out in the luncheon hour to put his cross on a ballot paper discriminating between candidates he did not know, in an election whose real issues it would be very hard to understand if they ever had any meaning. Yet the chain is there, and the fact that it is there is a continuous recognition that each voter counts, that his or her personal wishes to choose, however ineffectively, what may happen and to applaud or condemn, however ignorantly, what has happened, are matters to which attention must be paid.

Clearly this recognition of the inherent integrity and value of the individual man or woman as an individual human being is the key point. Upon it the difference in intention between the liberal and the totalitarian States turns; it is dimly represented in the characteristic traditions and institutions of the liberal States, and when we come to the difficult problems of freedom this principle will supply the test. It is of course the staple of much political oratory; indeed, it may seem to be so trite and obvious that it is wearisome to have to repeat it.

Yet though it may be trite it is not obvious. We have repeated it so often that we have forgotten how difficult it is to believe. In all countries and in all classes there are people who seem to have little or nothing to offer in terms of any accepted system of values; they are not wise, or beautiful, or interesting, or agreeable, or useful; they contribute little to the present and nothing to the promise of the future. To conceive that they have inherent value, that what they say or do ought to have the protection of an intricate organization, which may impede the development of a society in which better types might have a wider scope to develop, requires a system of thought which takes account of something else than the obvious values which present themselves to the mind. It could be grounded on the old conception of natural rights, though the philosophy which used to justify that idea is largely obsolete. What is germane to present purposes is that the idea can be converted into theological terms. The humane tradition can be considered to be the impartial love and mercy of God trying to penetrate human society; the tradition of justice to be an attempt, albeit an unsuccessful attempt, to reproduce the universal justice of God; all may be summed up in the principle, which I mentioned earlier on, that all men and women are alike the children of God and have equal value in His sight. It is along those lines that the principles of liberal democracy must make their claim to endorsement by the Christian religion.

It is indeed only for the principles, the intentions, behind their institutions or traditions that the divine sanction can be claimed. Their operation in the world of fact may fall far short of their intention and be rightly condemned. Nor is it possible to claim the sanction of Christianity for the particular institutions in any country which are designed to carry these intentions into effect. It would be absurd to say that I have thought things out as a Christian man and I now know that the quickest way to the station is by taking a particular short cut and that you are defying Christian principle if you believe that you can get there more speedily by another route; that would be an attempt to enforce my calculations on purely secular matters by invoking the sanction of religion, though a great many of the pronouncements which religious people make upon politics do, on analysis, do this very thing. So too in relation to liberal democracy. It seems possible to say that in the relative humanity of its traditions can be discerned the mercy of God, in its attempt to maintain the rule of law there is something of the justice of God, in the idea of government with assent there is some respect for the children of God. What it is not possible for me to say is that it is in accordance with the will of God that these intentions should be carried into effect by the particular institutions which commend themselves to me, by law-courts with independent judges and juries, or by free elections, or by any other political contraption, however solemnly commended by antiquity, or plausibly by calculation. I personally believe that these expedients are the best way of safeguarding these intentions, but my belief is based on my reading of history and my judgment of probabilities which no other Christian is bound to accept simply because he is a Christian. In fact there may be situations in which these calculations may not be correct.

There may, however, be one principle or intention in liberal democracy or in any form of democracy which no Christian may accept, much less commend. A basic idea in the theory of democracy has been that of the sove-reignty of the people: the phrase has been variously inter-preted, indeed the word sovereign is an equivocal word to which rather different meanings are from time to time ascribed; at the lowest, however, the conception of the sovereignty of the people would seem to mean that the decree of the majority is final and must be obeyed. But for Christians no human decree can be final, for all obedience to human authority must be conditional on its compatibility with the superior claims to obedience of the will of God. For no human sovereignty must rival the sovereignty of God.

This, indeed, is only one phase of an old and very bitter problem. Since the beginning of history at any given moment at any given place where organized life has gone on there has existed a power whose commands made such life a possibility. To use the word 'sovereign' of this power might raise technical difficulties; suffice it to say that in a large sphere of life it claimed absolute obedience as its due. That power normally was held to embody what at that moment seemed to be of the highest importance in human affairs. In the remote past it was no doubt the tribe or the city or the empire, mystically considered. At other periods it was hereditary right: either the hereditary right of a good many individuals to particular properties and privileges and the laws and customs which sanctioned that right, or the hereditary right of the single individual to give order to the whole. With us at the moment it is the assent and confused intention of the majority, for the will of the people can mean little more than that. Since at the moment the national group is the best vehicle for popular government, the power to be obeyed is held to embody the will of a particular nation, the will of, say, the British or French or Danish nation within its own territory. Possibly in the future it might be conceived as the will of some international confederation; also possibly in the future the power might be that of a technocracy, the right to rule of those who have been trained in a certain way and possess certain skills which are held to be necessary for the improvement of the life of mankind or even for the existence of mankind, organized in a hierarchy designed to give effect to those skills.

Unless completely predatory and destructive, this power has had in general considerable moral claims to the obedience of its subjects, for it has been by its means that they were able to live an organized existence. However, once some sort of universal morality has been conceived, it has also been conceived that there must be a limit to that obedience, a limit which the government may not recognize. This issue is as old as the *Antigone* of Sophocles, but it has reappeared in various guises at different times throughout Christian history, and it is not resolved by extending the governing power from a group or an individual to include everyone. It is still impossible for Christians to give unqualified obedience to any earthly power, however full and fair are the methods by which the will of the majority has been ascertained, however numerous they are who compose it. To a man who believes in God it cannot usurp His place; somewhere there must be a point of refusal, for in the last resort any earthly obedience must yield before obedience to His commands, sincerely conceived.

This is tolerably obvious in theory. It would be more obvious in practice if the power claimed by the earthly ruler was likely to be what might be called the rights of wilful sovereignty, that is, the right to decree a morality which its subjects had to accept whatever its relations to any universally accepted code of morals might be; for most people, not absolutely confused, would recognize at once that it is not in the power of the majority to say what shall be right and what shall be wrong. The issue, however, is seldom as simple as that, for men normally shrink from making a claim as crude as that. What they normally claim is a reasoned obedience for the ostensible object of obtaining some ideal end which all must accept —the greatest happiness of the greatest number, the future welfare of millions of people scientifically planned, the security of the nation, the preservation of a way of life, or of individual liberty, including the liberty of Christians to practise their religion: only of course the reasoning must be done by those who command and not by those who are to obey. If the object to be pursued, or the means chosen, do not commend themselves to the subject, he must nevertheless still obey, or suffer for his refusal.

This claim is not unreasonable, and it is morally defensible. If a man accepts the advantages of living in an organized community, he must accept also the disadvantages of such a life, and those disadvantages include the fact that he must either perform the duties which the power that gives order to the community believes to be necessary for its safety and welfare, or he must be punished for refusing to do so. This is a harsh dilemma, but I see no way to avoid it. If a state has a moral right to exist, a state has a duty to exist, and it cannot permit its existence to be menaced by the private opinions of a minority of its members; nor ought it to allow private opinions to enable men and women to escape arduous duties or disagreeable necessities which should be equally shared by everyone who is taking advantage of the order it affords. On the other hand, in the last resort a man or woman must follow his or her conscience, and take the consequences.

The situation can be mitigated if the government remembers that the object of government, at least of liberal government, is as far as is practicable to preserve freedom for its subjects, and if the dissident does not forget that the proper use of freedom is to serve others and to do what is necessary for their well-being. Moreover, the fourth commandment will be the less often broken if the government remembers that what it is attempting to enforce as necessary for men and blameless before God is only, at best, what is in its opinion necessary for men and blameless before God, and if the dissident remembers that what he resists is, at worst, only what is in its opinion forbidden by God. These are, however, only mitigations. The harshness of the dilemma lies in the conditions of life; and it would not be honest to pretend that the most earnest reflection on these, or any other considerations, will ensure that either side can escape it.

Since, however, the origin of this dilemma lies in the conditions of life, it is not peculiar to democracy. It existed before men conceived the idea of democracy, and will continue even if that idea is abandoned. All that need be said here is that the acceptance of democracy, however liberal, cannot exorcize it. The basis of morality cannot be arithmetical; it is not possible to free the individual from his duty, if he must, to resist the commands of the community by multiplying to any number those whose assent has endorsed those commands. It can, however, be added that in the respect which it has normally shown for the dissident and the conscientious objector the liberal State has certainly shown more care for the consciences of its subjects than any other form of government that exists today, possibly than any form of government that has existed before in history. In this matter it may be claimed that the development of its tradition has up to date encouraged an increasing recognition of the rights of the individual conscience to resist secular pressure, and so an increasing recognition of the sovereignty of God who rules through men's consciences.

This is a partial claim, a relative claim and an uncertain claim. We have no right to claim that the individual conscience is even as adequately protected as the necessities of the State might permit; we should be fools if we believed that we had eliminated the possibility of an unavoidable conflict between State necessity and the individual conscience; we have no reason to believe that in all circumstances or on all occasions in liberal democracies the integrity of the individual conscience is respected at all. But we may not make any other than partial, relative and uncertain claims on behalf of any of our traditions or institutions. All that we can say is that in the development of some of our traditions, the traditions which for instance condemn the brutalities in our own past and the savageries which have been practised in Germany and Russia and in China, can be seen the operation of the spirit of God, and that in the intention of some of our institutions can be seen a recognition of the law of God. We may go no further.

Yet it is important to realize that for many valuable people such partial, relative and uncertain commendations would be meaningless, if not disloyal. For many people all the time and, I think, most people part of the time, think by association and not analytically. They may use the big words democracy, freedom, justice, but the meaning they attach to them is not a precise abstract idea whose meaning and implications have been worked out in theory. The abstract meaning is vague and loose if it is present at all, though the feeling may be strong, and the conception may be strengthened by an impression of value experienced but not abstracted and analysed, or by a picture with which the idea is associated, as of the kind of community which supports or denies it, or of the kind of person who cultivates or rejects it, or of events in which the idea or its opposite seems to be displayed. This often happens, for the pull from the abstract to the concrete, from the general to the personal, is very strong indeed, and for some men and women political ideals have come to be expressed almost wholly in concrete terms, as in 'the American way of life', with which for many citizens of the United States the idea of democracy has become inextricably confused, or 'the British way and purpose' or some such phrase, which expresses for many Britons ideas about justice and humanity which seldom seem to rise above the instinctive level, or 'French civilization', which means for many Frenchmen all civilization. That does not mean that the idea has no meaning, only that it is expressed in a form in which it can be understood; indeed, it may gain in realism by being so expressed, as it gains greatly in the power of survival. For if it gains an association with something a man values—his family, the kind of people he instinctively likes and trusts, his mates in the factory, his religion, his country—it will be defended with an emotional force which does not often come from abstract enthusiasms.

In the late autumn of 1939 my father, while walking round some allotments near Leeds, fell into conversation with a very young private soldier. In due course my father asked him for what he believed he was going to fight. The boy thought over the matter carefully and then said: 'For my home.' Now this might seem to be an inadequate answer from one who was going to take arms and risk his life in one of the most important ideological struggles in history, but my father thought that it was a very good answer, and so it was. The best and most important factors in the boy's life were connected with his home; that home was truly threatened and he was going to play the man and defend it. With his home there may have been associated in his mind more general values of vital moment for humanity which were also threatened— kindness, fair dealing and the sanctities of private life—or there may not. But whatever is the truth of that, it was as well that he thought as he did, it was as well that he and many others responded to those simple loyalties; for, it may be asked, how many people in the supreme crisis of 1940 were prepared to risk what they risked for abstract political principles alone? I think the answer is, not very many, particularly in the countries which were not then attacked. I think that very many of the men and women who did in fact stand fast and resist the enemy were in their own view fighting for 'home', or that there should 'always be an England'. Yet if they had not done so the spirit of Auschwitz and Treblinka might very well have prevailed upon the earth.

These profound and elementary feelings, these primary loyalties, are deeply to be respected; round them is entwined much that is most valuable for mankind. Indeed, to judge by history, most general values need the force of these elemental powers to sustain them if they are to survive. Yet they can be very easily exploited for evil ends.

It is sad to think that in 1939 there may have been German boys who had thought things out and who also believed that they were fighting for 'home'. Of course, if they believed this they were mistaken; their homes had not been in peril, but they were to be imperilled by the power that was leading them, which also defiled the Germany that they loved. It would, however, be difficult for them to realize this. Much of the German propaganda played on these primary feelings, and the extraordinary toughness of the ordinary German troops, even perhaps the hesitations and divisions of some of those who opposed Hitler, may well show the power of the primary loyalties which he was able to exploit for his own wholly evil purposes.

In fact the compulsive power of a man's primary loyalty, of any primary loyalty—to home or country or class—is exceedingly strong, and it can carry a man into very strange company and very strange paths; and the values which he has associated with it can be dragged after him. I tried to suggest in my last chapter how often this has happened to various versions of the Christian religion; it can also happen to secular ideals which have become associated with some primary loyalty so intimately that the original idea is lost. It is interesting, for instance, to compare the emotional appeals made to the values of American life in the speeches of the men who exploited the issue of security in the United States, with their absolute disrespect for the provisions and objects of the constitution of the United States, in which those values are summed up. Even the great emotive words themselves—'liberty', 'justice', 'democracy'—can become mere vehicles for feeling, coins whose image and superscription have been rubbed off by much use but which have retained their value; and they can be appealed to to enforce action which denies the very things they were supposed to mean.

For this reason it is not only an intellectual duty to analyse strictly the meaning of words, it is a moral duty; as it is also a moral duty to reconsider continually and carefully to what extent the institutions and practices which are associated with them translate their intention into the world of fact. This is peculiarly necessary if we are to claim the support of the Christian religion for our ideas and institutions in the great debate. For the certainty of human failure must be assumed in the working out by men of any ideal, in the operation of any institution; and that failure will also certainly defile the conception of the ideal itself. However exalted it may be, or however sure may seem to be its divine warrant, every ideal will be distorted in some way or other by the human beings who paint its picture for the world, or for themselves. Indeed, it would seem to be true that the pride and selfishness of men penetrate so easily and so habitually even into abstract, analytical thought that no ideal, no institution upon earth, State or Church, can have the right to claim that as it is presented by men it embodies in every respect the undoubted will and purposes of God.

I believe the theologians of the Eastern Orthodox Church sometimes talk of something which they call the 'apophatic principle'. It is the 'negative way', the principle of realizing the incompleteness of every statement that a man makes as soon as it is uttered, the falsity of every idea that human frailty can frame, the imperfection of every human cause or institution, the probability of sin in all the movements of the human heart. This principle must be applied to all human creeds, democracy or theocracy, internationalism or patriotism, or quietism, that is, the rejection of secular commitments in favour as it might seem of purely spiritual values. It must be applied in particular to those things which a man rates highest and which he most loves and admires.

This last condition is a harsh one, but it is very important; important among other reasons because there is a substitute for the apophatic principle, a kind of holy snobbery which sometimes leads men and women to despise the ordinary virtues and the common traditions and aspirations of the society in which they live. On these they turn their satire because they enjoy so doing, or because it seems to enhance the idealized claims of a society or cause of which they are advocates. But this is not the apophatic principle, it is more normally pride; like all forms of snobbery it is a mean contempt for common things because they are common. It may lead to the miserable condition in which a man accepts all that a society can offer and yet takes pleasure in condemning the very means by which at great cost to other people these things have been secured for him. The antidote for this temptation is to love what one must criticize if one criticizes what one should love; it is to serve where that is possible, even at the expense of life, and yet to say 'God is not here, He is not in this', or rather, which is harder, 'He is here, but He is not here, He is in these things, but He transcends them and condemns them'.

It is not to be pretended that the tasks required are easy or painless. For instance, it is necessary to try to discover the reality behind all the convenient plausibilities of this world, to penetrate the comfortable optimism which is apt to conceal the true working of a valued institution, the easy phraseology which hides the inadequacy of a cherished idea, and to inquire into matters about which one's friends are complacent and resentful of inquiry, and about which one would much prefer to be satisfied oneself. Above all things it is necessary to search one's own mind to try to detect the concealed self-interest, the vanity, the reverence for one's own habits which lurk hidden in all one's ideals; and when all these things have been done they must all be done over again, for the tendency to mask fact by treasured fantasy is perennial and incurable. Yet these things must be done if we are to dare to claim that anything that we value has, however remotely, the sanction of Christianity; and they must be done if we are not to be deceived as (it is clear from the record of history) a great many good men have been horribly deceived.

This discipline is necessary in order that men should avoid the sin of idolatry, that they should not conceive their own desire or mistake to be the will of God, and in the place of God worship an idol of their own devising. Such discipline is continually necessary in all matters with which man is deeply concerned, but it is peculiarly necessary for the safety of mankind that it should be applied to the loyalties and ideals which lay claim on the allegiance of large numbers of human beings; for it is, after all, the public idols, civil or ecclesiastical, that have required most blood to be shed, most hearts to be broken, in their service.

But the fact that such discipline must be applied to our feeling for any secular institution, idea or system of politics ought not to mean that it is impossible for them to claim some support for the Christian religion in the great debate. After all, the virtues claimed on their behalf need not be so much absolute as comparative. It is not necessary to say that the liberal democracies present the will of God and nothing else, or that they are in any respect a perfect realization of the will of God, or that God could not fulfil Himself in other ways. Obviously it would be extremely wrong to say any of these things. But all that need be said is that in the possession of this or that institution, in the intention to obey and realize this or that principle, the liberal States possess something which reflects the will of God as it is not reflected in the intentions or the principles or the institutions of the States which are totalitarian. And if evidence were required to suggest that this claim was a probable one, it can be found in the facts of history and in the conditions of life in Russia and its satellites.

It is true that the appeal to history and the appeal to existing conditions must necessarily be in some sort unfair. What a State does, what happens in a community, are not by any means solely dictated by the type of institution which has been developed in it, the type of principle which it has inherited; these things themselves are in fact very heavily influenced by circumstances, which are different in every community. Indeed, the generalization might be hazarded that security and wealth induce freedom and mercy, and danger and poverty harshness and tyranny. Most of the totalitarian countries have been backward countries, or countries in peculiar difficulties, as was Germany in 1932; that was at least in part why they became totalitarian. On the other hand, the liberal States have been prosperous countries with a history of reasonable prosperity. This does not, however, remove the importance of the point of principle. The instinct for tyranny and cruelty does not only spring from danger and poverty; and there are philosophies which do not teach respect for the integrity of the individual in any circumstances. A study of the Nazi movement before 1930 suggests that Germany's economic difficulties were not the only reason why she became totalitarian. There is much in communist philosophy from before 1917 to explain the nature of the Soviet régime in Russia without reference to the backwardness of the country and the difficulties of its condition in the years that followed. Perhaps the fact of the matter is that the harshness of circumstances may explain why a particular philosophy triumphs over a country, but it does not explain the nature of that philosophy; and that raises this issue: supposing the pressure of circumstances relaxed, that poverty was mitigated and peace made secure, would a totalitarian state relax and guarantee freedom and justice and the dignity of man where those things are not now guaranteed? The answer seems to be that there is no reason either in their philosophy or in their practice up to date to lead one to believe that they would do so.

There is, however, a further point to be made of some importance. If a moral judgment is to be made, it must be

based on tradition, on institutions, on political philosophies, in fact on the issues of the great debate and not on
men and women. If things go wrong in the world, if ugly
things are done, it is hard indeed not to believe not only
that some living persons must be wholly responsible but
that we know who they are; or if we do not, that we do
at least know the kind of person likely to be responsible.
Sometimes, this attribution of guilt is associated with a
mental picture of a sinister individual, of which the con-
ventional ugly caricatures of national types are a crude
example: the cruel yellow-faced slit-eyed Chinaman who
has been of such use to sensational novelists, the sallow
and oily Italian ecclesiastic who was a stand-by of the
Protestant propagandists, the bulging Prussian who has
so often appeared in French and English cartoons, or the
callous Englishman with his protruding teeth and frigid
expression. Sometimes (often, no doubt) the feeling is
more subtle and less material, merely perhaps the prompt-
ing of the mind that, because one dislikes a political
philosophy or a course of action, it is necessary to dislike
and condemn those who must be its agents, for which
purpose one probably forms some mental picture of what
they are like, a picture which is not likely to have much
relation to fact.

But there is no necessity to deal in personalities; it is
the philosophy, the principle, the practice which matter,
not the agents. In actual fact the exact attribution of
moral responsibility is for human beings an exceedingly
difficult matter, which human beings had much better
leave well alone. That is something which I wish to argue
not here but in my sixth chapter. What I wish to do here

is to exclude an issue which I hold to be irrelevant. It is not our task to condemn the agents, prophets or dupes of the totalitarian state, as it is not our task to commend the virtue of those people who may have inherited a better tradition, which they did not create; even if those people happen to be ourselves.

It is the tradition which matters, and the philosophy it enshrines and the institutions which attempt to protect it; and if that tradition teaches some respect for the rights, integrity, and individual value of men and women, a Christian can see in it the operation of the spirit of God. For justice, humanity and freedom surely have their place in the law of God, and any attempt, however feeble, to secure them ought to have the sanction of His name.

Or rather, the case for humanity and justice is clear, but what about freedom? Freedom is peculiarly important because it is the characteristic principle of the liberal States. Now the conception of freedom seems to present two problems: the first, whether that conception is based upon realities which modern thought can accept and modern practice is likely to sustain; the second, whether the right to secular freedom is endorsed by, or is even compatible with, a belief in the Christian religion. I will deal with the first of these questions in my next chapter and with the second in the one that follows.

CHAPTER IV

FREEDOM

IN this chapter I want to deal with some part of a very large problem: to what extent is the idea of freedom, which is so important in politics, compatible with modern secular thought? I must attack it, but I cannot hope to deal with it adequately; for it is not only large, it is very difficult and touches on sciences such as psychology and philosophy in which I do not claim to have any skill.

Part of the difficulty lies in the word itself: to some, to many, it means too much; it has become so overcharged with special meaning that their use of it is to a misleading extent different from any ordinary usage. To others, in I think conscious contradiction to this, it probably means too little. To the first the state of freedom is necessary for the realization of certain important moral values. They are therefore inclined to include in the meaning of the word itself a realization of those values and even the conditions necessary for their realization; as, for instance, in the statement that 'freedom means knowledge of the moral law'. Often this kind of use is distinguished by particular adjectives. There is talk of 'real' freedom, or 'true' freedom, and in most cases these words secure that the word means something different from what the ordinary man means by freedom, and the use leads to confusion. Others, on the other hand, may be inclined to dismiss the word freedom as simply what they call a

'Hurrah word', a word exciting emotional enthusiasm without possessing any objective meaning. Even were that true, it would still be necessary to inquire why it excited this emotional enthusiasm; but it does not seem to be true, for the word seems to have in ordinary speech a perfectly clear, and reasonably simple, objective meaning.

As I see it, freedom always stands as the link in an equation, I am free *from* something *to* do something or be something. My arms are, as you see, not tied to my body, my hands are free *from* bonds and therefore I am free *to* wave them about. Both sides of the equation can always be found on analysis, but they are not always expressed. Sometimes they are not expressed because they are so obvious that they need not be expressed, sometimes because they appear to be so general that they can hardly be expressed. For instance, I am free *from* gout and therefore I am free *to* dance the cachucha, *to* drink port, *to* live my life without experiencing some types of pain—but I need not extend the list. On the other hand, I am free *to* breathe, but I hope the forces which might prevent me from breathing are so remote and unlikely that I need not speak of them.

There may, however, be a danger in not filling in both sides of the equation, because in fact what stands on the 'from' side governs what stands on the 'to' side; if what is on the 'from' side is defective, then what stands on the 'to' side will be defective also. For instance, I might say I am free *to* buy a Rolls-Royce motor car, and it is perfectly true that I am free *from* any legal disabilities which might prevent me from buying a Rolls-Royce. This, however, covers only part of the ground: there remain to be considered the state of my finances and the absurd prejudices of my bankers; and as a result of these things I am not free to buy a Rolls-Royce motor car. In not a few cases the context and obvious intention of the statement make clear what is meant to stand on one or other side of the equation. If I say that I am free *to* publish what I please I obviously mean that I am free *from* the operations of a censorship or some other form of legal or political interference which might in other circumstances prevent me from publishing certain statements; I do not mean that the publishers or printers will take any rubbish that I please to inflict on them. In some cases the intention of the statement is considered to be so obvious that it is not thought to be necessary to fill in either side, as in the statement that 'the Swiss are a free people'. This use, however, may lead to the danger that neither the reader nor perhaps the writer may really know what the statement means, which is always unfortunate.

On the 'to' side there is likely to be an element of choice: I am free *to* do something or not *to* do it, as I think fit. But on the 'from' side there may very well have been no choice at all: it may have been impossible for the individual to liberate himself; indeed, he may not in his enslaved condition have desired to be free. For instance, I am now free *to* read, I am free *from* illiteracy. Now that freedom was imposed on me when I was very young by the mild coercion of a certain number of patient women, starting with my mother. I was forced to be free, and the freedom conferred on me was a very real freedom. I can now do other things to the printed page than stare at it angrily and scribble over it with coloured chalks, though I could do that if I wanted to. I am free *to* read or not to read as I think fit; I am free *to* read rubbish or sense. Indeed, of all the freedoms that I enjoy, the one then imposed on me against my will is among the most precious. Yet there is one choice that that operation has forever denied to me: I am not free to return to my virgin illiteracy. As far as that goes this is a proposition about freedom in which neither on the 'from' side nor the 'to' side is there left any element of choice at all.

This consideration raises, or so I believe, certain profoundly important moral considerations, for to many people choice is an essential element in morality. To them (and I number myself among them), if an action is to have moral value, it must be to some extent the free choice of the actor. If he is compelled to perform it, it may be intrinsically valuable in some ideal scale, but there is no moral value in it for him. Indeed, it is this element of choice which gives its moral value to the principle of freedom; but if a man is forced to be free and that action has absolutely limited his choice in certain decisive directions, it may well be that this conception of moral value may be in danger.

The dilemma can be put in the terms of a very well-known religious difficulty. Supposing I suffered a religious conversion, I should then be free *from*, or freer than I now am *from*, a number of crippling, limiting things—*from* doubt, error, evil concupiscence and malice—and by all accounts should be freer *to* be myself, *to* serve God, which we are told is the only perfect freedom. But it is unlikely that I should also be freer *to* be evil, or *to* do evil; on those points my choice would, probably, not have been enlarged but restricted. Now certain religious teachers whose experience has been much deeper than our own have been insistent on the fact that this liberation can only come from the grace of God, that the will of man is utterly helpless even to choose to be free. But the result of the liberation also limits a man's choice, if it does not deny him any choice whatsoever in certain directions. The eternal lover takes the soul of a man who cannot choose but love and obey.

Thus no doubt he gains the glorious liberty of the sons of God. But if this account is true, it means that the terms 'freedom' and 'liberty' may require in certain contexts rather careful reconsideration, and it is I think significant that a good many people have been profoundly dissatisfied with this view. They have felt that it could not be a complete account of God's dealings with the human soul, that it was incompatible with their fundamental belief that both in the idea of freedom, and of moral value, a real element of choice was inherent; and they have felt that their own experience enforced that view. They have also believed that, if conversion or salvation are of supreme importance to a man or woman, it is incompatible with that justice which they have believed to be one of the attributes of God that God should deny them to one man and impose them on another.

I am not capable of discussing such matters, but I wish to suggest that at a very much lower level something of the same problem emerges from the relationship of an individual to the community in which he lives. The community also in some sort forces a man or woman born in its bounds to be free. To a greater or less extent it imposes on them the standards of a civilized community; it frees them from savagery or barbarism. As the State has increased in its sense of its responsibility towards its subjects, the amount of liberty that it imposes on them increases also. It imposes on them an increasing amount of education, thereby liberating them from the crippling effects of illiteracy. It imposes on them sanitary standards and medical precautions, thereby freeing them from certain diseases. It imposes on them standards of housing, conditions of employment and compulsory insurance, thereby freeing them from conditions which have hampered life or threatened its security.

In all these matters it is right and necessary to think of the compulsive work of the State as also a work of liberation. To emphasize the point it is only necessary to think of the condition of an inhabitant of a cellar in the Manchester of the 1840's, the Manchester described by Engels. He was housed in unspeakable conditions, he was normally hungry, he was at the mercy of ruthless economic forces, he was the prey to disease, and he was darkened by ignorance. It is true that the State interfered with his life much less than the State would do today, but taking this into account we may well ask, what freedom did he enjoy, and what was it worth? The answer may be that he enjoyed more freedom than we think and its worth from an eternal point of view may have been incalculable; that freedom was however not conferred on him by the lack of State action, and from a human point of view the most precious freedom society accorded to him would seem to have been very often the freedom to get drunk when there was money enough, which was, as was said, the shortest way out of Manchester. Since then, of course, the change has been incalculable. Part of the change has, no doubt, come from the general enrichment of the community, part from self-help and the mutual organization of labour. But, as a matter of plain historic fact, very much of this improvement has of necessity been organized by the community and imposed on those who benefited from it, not even at the dictation of a democratic vote. But the result has been to free men and women from the effects of their environment, to enable them to live more nearly the lives which men and women ought to live.

There may be a remote analogy here to the effects of religious conversion, but there are two important differences. The standards and ideas which the community imposes are those of men, they are not directly from God; they might not be from God at all. Nor is the order which the community imposes on the lives of men entirely moral or entirely the result of a change of heart, and therefore some coercion remains necessary to keep it effective. Therefore, obviously, certain rather important questions are posed. How far ought this process to be pressed? How far is one set of human beings justified in imposing its ideas on another set of human beings? How much coercion ought to be applied? Is there a point at which the coercion of the State is so effective and continuous that its result is not to produce freemen but slaves?

These are basic questions, and not easy ones; however, I believe they cannot be considered until a further question has been asked and answered, if an answer is possible. How much can be done to change and control men and women by manipulating the forces working on them from outside? I had almost said, in posing this question, 'by changing their environment'; but the word 'environment' might seem only to refer to what might be called physical conditions: the housing available, the state of the towns and villages, the conditions and rewards of employment, or the control of health or disease. Clearly there is much else in question here, there is the provision of education and the control of its content, the control of propaganda and the sources of information, in fact the moulding to some desirable plan of all the mental and spiritual factors which affect the development of the human mind.

No man can, I believe, study history at all seriously without reaching the conclusion, desired or undesired, that the power to change human beings by changing their environment is very great indeed. There seems to be little question that the physical conditions in which a man lives do affect a man's character, though it is probably less easy to say how they affect it than it is sometimes held to be. I believe also that there should be as little question that a man draws most of his ideas from his mental environment, which can be very largely controlled by exterior forces, though, as far as I have been able to study the matter, the conclusion has been forced on me that the way in which this environment is built up is a far more subtle and complicated process than any historical description of it yet achieved has been able to suggest. It is in fact probably the next and most important task of historians to go much more deeply into that matter. But the questions to be considered here are these. Is it possible that this environment, mental and physical, does in fact control the whole of a man? And if this is so, is it possible, or is it going to be possible, that this environment can be so manipulated by statesmen that the human beings in their charge can be absolutely and finally changed into what they desire?

There are strong reasons which must lead almost any man of good will to hope passionately that this may be so. If the factors in men's environment which lead to violence, crime, disorder and discontent could be abstracted, then the element of force which is now a necessary but terrible part of the ordering of the world's affairs could be progressively eliminated too. It is true that no one has yet been able to reach this point, but that may be because they have as yet had insufficient knowledge or an insufficient control of material resources, or minds that were not sufficiently clear, or wills that were not sufficiently strong to do what was necessary. But the possibility may still be open; indeed, unconsciously or consciously, it forms the background of a vision which haunts humanity. A rather crude version of this vision is the Marxist dream of a classless society from which the causes of social conflict have been eliminated by the simplification of its economic structure in which the coercive State may wither away. It may be doubted whether anyone now really believes in the vision in this naïve form. Nevertheless, it is probable that the vision still floats in some form, more vague, more tentative but still infinitely attractive and alluring, at the back of the mind of almost every man who thinks and feels.

If economic resources were effectively organized and more scientifically developed and exploited than they are at present, it might well be possible to abolish poverty. If poverty went, crime might follow; if economic competition for insufficient resources were relaxed, war might go the same road. If human beings did not deem it to be necessary to set aside so much of their resources in absurdly wasteful preparations for the horrible business of killing other human beings, then the resources liberated for the enjoyment of mankind would increase, and its tensions would relax, and its insecurity disappear, and the attack on poverty and all its attendant evils could be re-invigorated with an ever-increasing momentum. It is true that these hopes are based on two unproved hypotheses: that crime is caused by poverty, and that war is caused by economic competition; indeed, the evidence that is available seems to contradict the truth of either assumption, particularly the second, as a complete account of the matter. Moreover, any schemes for universal amelioration must find some way of putting a stop to the prevailing tendency for population so to increase in certain parts of the world when there is any improvement of resources that the only result is that more people live in the same misery. Nevertheless, some of the causes of evil seem to be so patent and unnecessary that it ought not to be impossible for better and more universal education to enlighten men as to the manifest error of their ways; it is easy to dream that, if a series of sufficiently obvious facts were made sufficiently clear to a sufficiently large number of people, there should be no reason why the progress of mankind should not be universal, indefinite and uninterrupted. After a stormy morning the golden afternoon of mankind might commence, an afternoon which need fear no evening for a longer period than man has yet been a talking and planning animal.

We have all dreamed this dream, equipping our Utopia with this or that piece of machinery, or this or that universal idea which our fancy suggests to be necessary. It is not an ignoble dream, nor in every respect an impossible one. So much has been done, and we forget how much has been done, for the inhabitants of the advanced States of the world, that it seems clear that more can be done, and must be done, for them and for everyone. It is necessary to think clearly how this shall be; but in our waking moments we normally realize that any scheme for secure and universal happiness must control one unruly factor, which is not poverty, and is not ignorance, and whose vagaries do not all spring from easily diagnosed disease. It is the human will, or what appears to be the human will. There would appear at the moment to be no paradise which it cannot turn into hell, no simple and salutary lesson which it cannot, with passion, reject.

Perhaps we believe that this factor also can be controlled by wise and careful manipulation. But if this can be complete and final, then an important conclusion seems to be forced on the mind: that the will of man can be completely controlled by factors which lie outside him, and which are not in his charge. Indeed, the tendency is to go further and to say there is nothing within a man but what comes from his environment; alter that and you absolutely alter the man himself; that his wishes and his personality are only what his environment and his physical condition have made of him. But if that is so, what becomes of the moral value of the power of choice? And what happens to the philosophy of the liberal State which defends the power of choice? Has the whole thing been a pitiable delusion, the resolute and heroic defence of something which in fact could not exist? This, however, brings into the picture the two ugly words 'determinism' and 'materialism'; for if you believe that human beings can be completely controlled by manipulating their environment, it would seem that you must be a 'determinist'; and, to the extent that you believe that it can be done by modifying their material environment, you must be a 'materialist' as well.

They are indeed ugly words. They are very often used as terms of abuse, and they are equivocal; they very often pretend to a precise meaning which they do not possess. Yet behind them, in the shadow they cast upon discussion, there lurk very important ideas, often unanalysed or, often enough, confused tendencies of thought, often unrealized. It is necessary to come to terms with these words as best we may.

The root idea in determinism seems to be the denial that human beings have any power to choose freely. But this negative belief may be the result of a number of different positive beliefs which it is convenient to group into two categories. On the one hand, it may be believed that all human conduct is controlled by one, or perhaps one or two, agents which we know all about, and perhaps can ourselves control. This perhaps might be called 'simple', or even, in extreme cases, 'single-cause' determinism. On the other hand, it may be held that human conduct is controlled by a very large number of agents. Of some of these agents we may be ignorant. They may work in ways that we do not understand; indeed, the very words 'control' and 'cause' may themselves be philosophically suspect. But these agents must not include anything that can be recognized as the human will working freely as we have believed it to work. This might be called 'complex' or 'multiple', or, where that is suitable, 'agnostic' determinism.

From a political point of view, simple determinism is probably more dangerous than multiple or agnostic determinism. If you feel sure that the motives that direct mankind are reducible to a very short list and that you know what they are, you are probably likely to treat your fellows with less respect than if you are aware of the complexities and mysteries of human nature; this is particularly true if you believe that you yourself can manipulate these motives. But both sorts of determinism are destructive of morality, if free choice is an element in morality; and neither supports the case that the State ought to defend the power of freedom of choice, for each denies that such a power exists. The multiple determinist may feel that the task of handling his fellows is a more complex one, producing more difficult problems, than the cruder thinker will allow, but it seems that there can be for him no particular reason why he should not manipulate the minds of his fellows to suit his own convenience if he can do so. There is nothing for him to respect in the independence of the human personality, for that is a fantasy. This is perhaps a dangerous opinion in a century in which the technique of manipulating the human mind has developed so rapidly and in which it shows every sign of developing further.

Materialism as a word is even more equivocal than determinism. It could perhaps be applied to a whole spectrum of opinion in which the lines between different shades of meaning are not always very clearly defined. At one end of the spectrum is the bare assertion that matter exists and that all is not spiritual or conceptual (using all these words loosely and without definition). This view is of course generally held, except by the devotees of certain Eastern religions and by certain Western philosophers. On the whole, Christianity is probably committed to this view. Next to that in the spectrum comes the opinion that matter is important and significant and has important effects on what is spiritual, an opinion which would seem to be based on common experience and common sense. This view seems to be also possible for a Christian. Then comes the opinion that matter is predominantly important, and that what is spiritual is always subordinate to it; and next to that, that what is spiritual is wholly derivative from matter.

This last opinion is apparently the materialism that the communists accept. Stalin says that it is their philosophy; 'that matter is primary, since it is the source of sensations, ideas, mind, and that mind is secondary, derivative, since it is a reflection of being; that thought is a product of matter which in its development has reached a high degree of perfection, namely, of the brain, and the brain is the organ of thought'. But there is presumably a point even further down the scale in the spectrum than this: that is, the opinion that there are no such things as the spiritual or the mental at all, that the universe is no more than a mass of jarring atoms, combining, separating, recombining, under the impact of fortuitous currents, and all that happens takes its shape simply, as it were, as the result of the haphazard rotation of a monstrous kaleidoscope, even presumably the statement that makes such an assertion.

The situation is made more difficult by the fact that the word 'matter' is not easy to define and limit, and also by the fact that we are all probably too much accustomed to far too simple a division between soul and body, or mind and body, as separate entities. These are matters on which I have no right to an opinion at all, but I would say that this relationship is very complicated, more intimate than is normally implied; for on the one hand there is a great deal of evidence of the profound influence of bodily conditions on mental and spiritual conditions, and on the other hand there is much evidence, though it has been much less effectively investigated, of the influence of spiritual and mental conditions on bodily ones.

However, be that as it may, the more extreme positions in this scale seem to lead to two opinions. First, that free choice is impossible, for if mind does not exist and the material is predominant, clearly mind cannot choose. A man can be detached from one set of exterior conditions as a bag is detached from a hook, but only to be subjected to another set of exterior conditions as the bag falls to the ground under the control of gravity. Secondly, in a purely materialist universe there would seem to be no place for an absolute or transcendent system of values: there could only be at best a set of arbitrary desiderata in a universe in which everything is fortuitous. If these things were so the great debate would have to come to an end. For the case for the liberal democracies would be meaningless; there would be no values by which to judge that or any other case, and no independent minds to conduct any discussion.

In fact the results of the logic of such opinions would be alarming; but I believe there is no cause for alarm at this point, for a very simple reason. I do not believe that any human being has ever really believed in either of these extreme opinions. Men have believed in pretty rigid determinism for other people or even for themselves at particular moments; but when it comes to their own casual actions such as the crooking of a finger, or even to their power of framing observations and opinions, however effectively they have masked their belief, they have in fact believed that they have had some freedom of decision and judgment. For instance, they may have believed that they were compelled by the nature of objective truth to make this or that observation, but they have not believed that they were compelled by something exterior to themselves to say and believe all the things that they said or believed whether they were objectively true or false. If they held that opinion, there would be no grounds for making any observations at all, and then it is true discussion might as well come to an end. The same thing is, I believe, as true of the problem of an absolute set of values. In fact men always do accept the existence of an absolute set of values, and they try to prove that their actions and their theories comply with it. They need to appeal to such values to commend their own policies and stigmatize those of their opponents, as is amply proved by the expressive language of communist publicists in discussing the actions of people with whom the Russian government does not at the moment see eye to eye.

Of course there are a number of motives which make men want to take up a determinist position. For instance, men who have been exhaustively engaged in investigating the influence of one set of phenomena seem often to suffer from an almost irresistible temptation to expand their conclusions and erect them into rather crude systems of single-cause determinism. They become deeply impressed by the influence on human beings of economic conditions, geographical conditions, the power of race, the inevitability of the historic situation, the force of certain bodily needs and appetites, the importance of certain physiological or psychological conditions, and they become very anxious to say that here, in the power that they have discovered or displayed, is the unique mainspring of human conduct. Also, as is very natural, weak men who have done things of which they are ashamed wish to take refuge behind some form of determinism and claim that they could not help themselves. Conversely, strong men and strong women of very energetic wills like to feel that their actions are endorsed by some superhuman force which is larger than themselves, that they pronounce the will of God, that they are the sword of God, that they are the agents of history or of destiny, or that they are the scientific interpreters of the economic laws which must govern the world.

These are all emotional reasons for desiring to believe in some form of determinism, but it would be idle to deny that there are cogent rational reasons as well. If all the factors that control human conduct are taken honestly into consideration, it is difficult to find a place for freedom of the will as it has normally been understood. There are indeed difficulties in believing in the existence of the integrated human personality from which the will can proceed. And there are the special difficulties of the theologian confronted by the facts of the sovereignty and omniscience of God.

Nevertheless, I myself believe that none of these reasons ever lead men to act as if many of the actions of their lives were not under their control, and in fact and at bottom to fail to believe that they are under their control. And in this opinion, so I think, they reflect what is the truth of the case, obscure and complicated as the truth probably is. If men deny to mankind freedom of the will, they are, so I believe, denying to others a freedom which they know themselves to possess.

However, even though there may be no reason to be alarmed at the possibility of a rigorously logical acceptance of either determinism or materialism as a theory, there may yet be cause for alarm. The fact that a theory is intellectually inconsistent, or illogical, or incomplete, or not rigorously believed, does not mean that it will not affect the affairs of mankind. Marxist-Leninist communism seems to me to be confused on the subject of determinism, but that has not meant that the rulers of Russia have shown any greater respect for the freedom of choice either of their opponents or of their adherents. And it may well be that the determinism and materialism that we have to fear is something less logical and less explicit than Marxist-Leninist communism, something to be found in the unspoken assumptions of the pre-occupied man of action, the working hypotheses of the practical scientist who has not had much time or much use for abstract thought, or the everyday creed of the ordinary human being deeply immersed in the ordinary day to day business of life.

As has already been suggested, the conditions which lead to these attitudes are to be found outside the area in which communism is the official creed. It is natural that they should be prevalent. The need to organize material prosperity must be for many men an unceasing and in-evitable duty; after all, some modicum of that prosperity is necessary to maintain the values of society. Society cannot subsist, much less improve itself, on a romantic mixture of high ideals and economic failure. But absorp-tion in that task can lead to some impatience with claims that seem to impede its performance, and to some in-credulity about the values on which those claims are based. It is an impatience and incredulity of which symptoms can perhaps be seen in the ready, often wanton, destruction of natural or historic beauty, perhaps to secure some quite hypothetical material advantage, or in the sharp demand that higher education should become for more and more people nothing more than a training in useful technological skills with an increasingly per-functory and insincere lip-service to the value of the other endowments which education has provided in the past.

But perhaps this absorption is at its most serious when it leads men who are engaged in some important practical task, not merely to neglect the claims of the spiritual, but also to tend to deny the existence of certain human capacities, and perhaps to cease adequately to respect human rights. For instance, there is a tendency among medical men who are incessantly engaged in the task of dealing with the physical factors that affect human beings to reject the possibility of the importance of factors which are not physical as not worth consideration; this tendency may be responsible for the rather curious history of the problems of hypnosis in the nineteenth century, and another symptom of it may be the surprising light-heartedness with which some doctors seem to contemplate the responsibility of changing the personality of a sane man by the use of the surgeon's knife. Or in another sphere, psychologists engaged in dealing with the obsessions which distort the human personality have at least permitted currency to a popular view that all human beings are automatically controlled by mental fixations, and that personal responsibility is a fiction, an opinion of which the political implications and results will bear a good deal of consideration. And there is a school among lawyers who have come to see law as a functional science to be used to secure the smooth working of human relationships and to be impatient with the conception of law as a historic system devised to protect human rights.

In few cases, in all probability, has a fully developed philosophy been adopted, that is, one whose full implications in the ordering of human relationships have been properly worked out. In many cases professional absorption in a certain range of problems has led to the habitual acceptance of certain assumptions and to the neglect, and sometimes the dislike, of other considerations, and also indeed to the dislike of the evidence which might suggest that they ought to be taken into account. But the result may well be a way of thinking in which the values of liberal society have no sure foundation. No doubt the original motive is very often benevolent; there may even be a confused, or explicit, intention to secure human freedom. The ruthless development of modern technology is to secure freedom from want. Doctors are always struggling manfully to secure freedom from disease, psychologists to secure freedom from the effects of mental maladjustment, those who take the new view of law from the inefficiencies of an obsolete legalism. In each case the work may be estimable and valuable up to a point, but in each case it is necessary for human safety to make sure that the equation is completed—freedom to do what? to be what?

For the real answer may be only freedom to do or to be what the manipulators desire, and this in turn might mean that the man is to be free only to be a useful cog in an industrial machine, only to be the contented recipient of such material well-being as it may be convenient to afford to him, only to fill a suitable niche in the social machine which a streamlined law has organized, but to be content with that niche because he has been conditioned for the purpose by the increasingly efficient psychological and physiological techniques which a modern statesman has at his command.

All this may possibly add up in many cases to the freedom to be happy. It may well be that the use of these techniques may at last efficiently fulfil the great ideal of the greatest happiness of the greatest number. They will in fact be happy as beasts are happy. More obsolete values—the freedom to choose or to believe in a source of value which lies outside these arrangements—might easily prevent this fulfilment. Such ideas might well make men and women turbulent, unadaptable, discontented and miserable, as they have in fact often done in the past. And if it seems clear that men can in no case have freedom to choose, that that idea is meaningless and that there can be no exterior source of value, there seems to be no reason at all why any of these inconveniences need be permitted.

At the end of that passage there lie, as we all know, the modern nightmares, Aldous Huxley's *Brave New World* and George Orwell's *1984*. How serious is the threat to humanity which these suggest I do not know; no man can know. Clearly the danger is greater in the totalitarian State than in the liberal State; indeed, it is from the totalitarian State that Orwell seems to have drawn most of his subject-matter. Where the press, and scholarship, are reasonably free and not merely instruments for inculcating views which are convenient for the government, there will probably be a power which works for independence of thought. Where the courts maintain the tradition of individual right, there will remain some protection for individuals. Most important of all, where there is a strong tradition of personal freedom, there will remain strong personal prejudices against certain types of interference with men or women, or against their being subjected to too absolute a control.

Yet the forces which might modify our system of free-dom are, as we have seen, strong. The industrial con-dition of Great Britain is unsatisfactory: it might easily deteriorate. A more ruthless technological development, a more severe industrial discipline may very easily become a necessity. It may be necessary to accept a savage con-trol of consumer goods to divert resources to export or the replacement of capital; and in both cases the choice may very well be between these measures and starvation. There are other matters in which the controlled planning of the country may become increasingly necessary, and it has proved to be not at all difficult to by-pass the rule of law by legislation which increases the scope of adminis-trative powers. As more and more education draws its resources from public funds, more and more education will necessarily pass under public control, and the State might feel called upon to use more fully than it does now the power it possesses to control what is taught, par-ticularly when the cry for technological training becomes more insistent. And there are not a few other directions in modern society in which liberty could be progressively denied to individuals, not dramatically or intentionally or tyrannically, but piecemeal, unconsciously, kindly, with everyone acting with the best intentions. None of these things, of course, need destroy essential liberties, if men care about essential liberties and believe them to be extremely important; but they add up to a formidable total if they do not.

And it is important to remember this fact. Institutions are based on ideas, and if those ideas dry up the institu-tions may wither away like trees which have lost their sap. Two traditions seem to have helped to form liberal institutions. There was the belief which developed in the eighteenth and early nineteenth centuries in the ultimate identity of human interests. It was believed that if men were rightly informed and were freed from exterior interference, their desires would not clash but lead them to co-operate. Behind this was the more ancient conception of the natural and inherent rights of human beings. Now I think historical experience has shown that there was truth in the belief in the force of the ultimate identity of human interests, but not enough truth; it was for this reason that the nineteenth-century objective changed from the *laissez-faire* to the collectivist State. And the idea of the inherent rights of the individual seems to rest on a conception of value which was natural to a Christian or to a stoic or to a deist, and possible for an agnostic, but is meaningless to a dogmatic or practical materialist.

All this necessarily emphasizes the significance of the acceptance or rejection of Christianity for those who take part in the great debate. For a Christian must not only believe in a transcendent system of values, he must also believe in the inherent rights of all men and women as children of God. He cannot consider them simply as raw material to be used and moulded for the purposes of the community. Each severally must be an end in himself with a soul whose salvation depends in the last resort on either his own actions or on the grace of God, but not on the actions of other men. Therefore Christianity may perhaps provide a more secure basis for freedom than any of the other systems of thought which now prevail in the world. Again, however, the equation must be filled in: freedom from what? freedom to do what? to be what? Freedom *from* manipulation by the community, freedom *to* serve God and for no other purpose, for surely from the premise of the proposition freedom for any other purpose cannot be envisaged. But how does that presumption fit in with the conceptions of the liberal State? With that I will deal in the next chapter.

CHAPTER V

FREEDOM AND CHRISTIANITY

AT the end of the last chapter I tried to suggest what seems to me a dilemma about Christian freedom. On the one hand, the sanctions of Christianity are rightly invoked in favour of individual human freedom. On the other hand, if you fill in both sides of the equation, you appear to get this result: Christianity must demand for every man freedom *from* any secular control that negatives his individual value as a child of God and as a soul to be saved, but it does so only that he may have freedom *to* serve God and tread the way of salvation. To use that particular sanction to secure freedom for any other purpose would be rather like saying 'I must have this morning free to write a lecture, therefore you must leave me in peace to do the *Times* crossword puzzle.' Moreover, those who invoke the sovereignty of God against the authority of the State necessarily accept the fact that He must be sovereign over the subject too. They cannot claim that the State must be subordinate to Him but the subject independent: both must be absolutely subordinate. Therefore a man might be tempted to go on to say that it is not the totality of the secular totalitarian State which is wrong, but the fact that it is the wrong totality. Christianity also makes totalitarian demands, and therefore what is wanted is a Christian totalitarianism to set against the nationalist or communist totalitarianism on the other side of the line.

Perhaps such arguments do not appeal in the language which I have used. But the thoughts behind them have been common enough, sometimes instinctive, sometimes explicit. They have, or so I believe, led human beings into some of the most disastrous mistakes which have ever been made by human beings of good intention. For this reason it seems to be rather urgently necessary to think carefully about the problems emerging from two types of policy to which such thoughts have led: first, the attempt to use the power of the State to impose Christian morality on men's actions; second, the attempt to use the power of the State to impose Christian beliefs on their minds and to save them from being led astray by the delusive attractions of any competing system. Of these, the second offers the more difficult problems, for it does not deal with the direct control of action but with the instruction of the thoughts which will lead to action, and it is not so easy to see what is wrong with it.

However, the policy of the direct control of action has also to be considered. It has often been attempted, for there is a strong *prima facie* case in its favour. By its nature the State must impose some standard of conduct upon its subjects, and many people have believed that in a Christian country the standards to be imposed ought to be the standards of Christian morality. This belief has led to policies which varied from a general attempt to secure that the laws of Christian community corresponded where possible to Christian morality, rather loosely conceived, to a savage attempt to impose an exacting code of 'Christian' conduct with the aid of the prison, the whip and the gallows.

Even at their lowest and most temperate level, these policies easily lead to a dangerous mistake in morals. It is true that every system of law ought to be based on a code of morality, but to conceive that any code of morality is effectively represented by any working system of law is to contaminate the idea of that code of morality. The heavy-handed working of any police system, however excellent its traditions and rules, the unequal working of any human law, the fumbling clumsiness of all human justice, the harshness and unevenness of any human system of punishment, are all things which should not be confused with the operation of the law and power of God. If they are so confused, they degrade men's idea of God whether they assent to them or rebel against them.

However, as triumphant virtue becomes more savage and exacting, the situation generally gets much worse. At some point the virtuous normally begin to attempt to impose a morality which is different from that generally accepted by large sections of the population, and this leads to the law's being broken or evaded by reasonably right-minded people; this in turn leads to moral confusion, corruption and much dishonesty, as can be seen on a massive scale in the history of prohibition in the United States and to a less extent in the operation of the laws about street betting in England. As men go further and attempt to impose the routine of Christian life on everyone and to punish vice with exuberant fidelity, they normally increase two things, cruelty in the ruler and hypocrisy in the subject.

The ruler becomes cruel because he is clear that he is doing God's service and therefore need not trouble too much about such minor considerations as mercy, or justice, or respect for his brother man. The subject becomes hypocritical because he learns that what he needs to do is, not to fulfil the law of God, but to obey the laws or escape the vigilance of man; and since the severity of man masquerades as the will of God, the fear of the Lord comes to be the beginning of lying.

The reasons for all this should be obvious. Human discipline can indeed produce a situation in which a moral course of action is more probable than it would be without it; it can certainly make orderly and civilized conduct more likely and harmful conduct less likely. The fear of human coercion may go far to prevent certain atrocious actions, if it cannot prevent atrocious thoughts. It can in most cases prevent a man from killing his wife, if it cannot prevent him from wanting to kill her. It can prevent open physical cruelty, but can hardly touch covert mental cruelty. And neither disciplined habit nor the fear of punishment can provide the motives which alone make a moral action valuable. There is only one motive which enables a man to serve God, and that is, because he loves God, or loves the right, if the vision of God is denied to him. If men try to supply the place of this motive with fear, if they try to force men's actions in matters where moral assent is necessary, both sides are normally corrupted, and what appeared to be the work of God becomes very quickly the work of the devil. Indeed, this has happened very frequently both in the Christian State and in the Christian family.

The problem of freedom of opinion presents great difficulties. If the premise remains that men and women must be free to serve God, then it would seem to follow that it must be quite certain that they do know, as far as it is given to men to know, what are the purposes of God. It may well be the case that action ought, as far as is practicable, to be based on free choice. But ignorance and delusion do not lead to free choice: they lead to restricted choice, and in this case choice restricted at precisely those points at which it should be conscious and percipient.

There is much truth in this, it is worth much thought. The liberal answer to this problem is that men and women must be left free to find out the truths that are important to them. Christians may teach, indeed must teach, but they may not compel. Nor may they prevent any other men from teaching what they also believe to be true. Any truth, however sacred and however important, must be prepared to take its chance in that forum in which all sincere men have an equal right to speak.

Behind this answer there stretches a long chain of venerated authorities from before Milton to Milton, from Milton to Locke, from Locke to John Stuart Mill; and it forms the basis of a creed held by a variety of men whom everyone must view with respect. They would claim that all adult men and women ought to enjoy complete freedom of the mind based on free access to information—freedom to consider any point of view, and absolute freedom to express their own. These rights it would be said are an essential component of human freedom: to talk of freedom while refusing these rights would be a cynical and sinister abuse of terms. Therefore neither the government, nor public opinion, nor any Church, nor any other body, has the right to use its power to impose on men its own view of truth except by argument, or to deny currency to what it believes to be error. This view has not normally been based on any disbelief in the extreme importance of truth; on the contrary, those who have expounded it have often been distinguished for their belief that a sincere apprehension of truth, as far as men could compass it, was the only possible basis for right conduct. They have, however, felt assured that without free discussion the truth would certainly be distorted, but that probably in absolutely free discussion it would be progressively revealed, because of its intrinsic power to compete with its adversaries. 'Magna est veritas', they would say, 'et praevalebit'—which is a common and significant misquotation from the Vulgate.

It is a noble belief, it has been believed by noble-minded men, but the real question is: do we ourselves believe it? This absolute freedom may work satisfactorily for the chosen few who have the leisure to think and the education and power of mind which will enable them to think honestly and systematically; but complete freedom of discussion will extend its results to others who do not possess these powers and opportunities, but whose conduct and beliefs cannot be treated with indifference. Are all men and women to be granted these liberties even when it is notorious that they cannot make use of them?

For instance, are children to be allowed to choose their beliefs for themselves? Can they possibly make any effective choice? It may be said that their education should equip them to make their choice later on; but meanwhile all cannot be left tentative. Some definite doctrine must be taught them as a framework for their instruction; and in fact some definite and probably controversial doctrine will certainly be taught them with all the authority of an adult mind in contact with an undeveloped one. And what is taught in childhood will colour, and perhaps control, the choice of belief when the child is of an age to choose. That is why the control of the education of children presents such difficult moral and political problems. They are perhaps specialized problems; probably children must be excepted from the rules which, it may be, should prevail in the world of adults. But, to be honest, how far do these difficulties really cease with childhood? What power have the ordinary preoccupied man and woman, unused to systematic thought and uninterested in it, to criticize what is proposed to them with confidence about matters which are outside their own experience? Is it not the fact that they will accept their opinions either from one authority or from another? If that is so, does not our duty to them compel us to make sure that they are only instructed by those who will not lead them astray?

We talk of truth emerging from controversy, but, if one is frank, can one say that anything that is in the least likely to be true will necessarily emerge from the confused scuffle of public discussion that takes place in the world, with the demagogue, the quack, the skilled propagandist and the half-educated fanatic in full activity? And if one surveys the wild tangle of divergent convictions that riot over the inhabited globe, can one say, honestly, that any one body of recognizable truth has in fact done so? So much is imposed by environment, so much by the chances of education, ignorance accepts so much so readily from the dishonest, that an elementary right to be exposed to the free play of opinion must be for many no more than an elementary right to be deceived.

For many—or perhaps for all? For why should we be so sure that the educated few who occupy themselves with systematic thought should be immune from deception? Systematic thought seems to have led different men at different times to utterly incompatible conclusions, some of which may seem to us on reflection to be very odd indeed. Why should we rely with any confidence on the results of methods which they all believe themselves to have used and which have carried them so far in such divergent directions? The old philosophy from which the doctrines of freedom of opinion and discussion have derived relied on human reason as the last court of appeal; but how reliable is the procedure of that court, and how trustworthy are its findings? The men of the early eighteenth century who deified human reason normally relied on a simple psychology in which no one could now believe, and indeed their belief often degenerated into a childish self-confidence which tested everything by the short measuring-rod of a singularly limited common sense. Their methods did not give satisfaction for very long. They were challenged by the romantics in the name of the revelations of a deeper emotional experience; they were challenged in the name of religion by the evangelical and the catholic revival, and anyone who cares to read Newman's *Grammar of Assent* will, I believe, find in it how cogent are his arguments for another approach to truth. On the sceptical side they were also challenged by

Hume, and I believe that modern philosophy has effectively demonstrated the extraordinary difficulties that hamper ordinary human reason in its attempt to frame any proposition that has any meaning, or to ask questions which are questions at all. The problems of epistemology, the problems of the concealed but disputable premise, the problems of language, all seem to suggest how uncertain are the results of this court on whose findings our forefathers placed unquestioning trust.

Of course, if these analyses are pressed to their most devastating result, there would not seem to be any strong reason for going further into the matter. For who would accept martyrdom, who would even cross the road, to secure the right to say that the questions he wanted to ask were unlikely to be questions at all, and that it was improbable that anything he said would have significant meaning? In such case it would be better to abandon altogether the inconveniences of free discussions which lead nowhere, and to teach men doctrines which, even if they are on analysis absurd, would at least make them happy and useful. But if there is a chance that there is a truth which is more nearly coherent and more relevant to the conduct of human life than these analyses suggest, then perhaps authority of some sort should direct human minds to conclusions which free discussion and a confusing dialectic will never reveal to them.

There are, in fact, not a few people in the world today who believe that freedom of discussion is not likely to be of much advantage to human beings. There are non-Christians who believe that all the truths which are necessary for men have already been discovered, and that free discussion is only likely to lead to deviationism. There are also Christians. In his Encyclical *Immortale Dei*, published in 1885, Pope Leo XIII says: 'So also the freedom of thinking and of writing whatever one likes, without restraint, is not of itself an advantage at which society may rightly rejoice, but, on the contrary, a source of many evils.' He asserts that it is the duty of the State to give to the Christian religion, by which of course he means that form of Christianity in which he believes, the whole of its support and favour. He does, however, realize that in existing circumstances this cannot always be done 'The Church,' he says, 'it is true, deems it unlawful to place the various forms of worship on the same footing as the true religion: still it does not on that account condemn those rulers who, for the sake of securing some great good or preventing some great evil, allow by custom and usage each kind of religion to have its place in the State.'

A modern application of this teaching can, I think, be seen in present-day Spain. It is laid down in the charter of the Spanish people that the profession and practice of the Catholic religion is the official religion of Spain, but it is also stated that no one will be molested on account of his religious opinions, or in the private practice of his cult. No external ceremonies or manifestations, however, other than those of the Catholic religion are to be permitted. This should grant a limited, a very limited, toleration to Protestants in Spain; yet there is every evidence that even this amount of toleration has not always been fully enjoyed.

Since the civil war the authorities have not permitted certain Protestant chapels to be reopened, or where they have been opened they have in some places been closed by the authorities. Absolutely private worship has been interrupted. Protestant education has been made difficult since Protestant schools have been closed, and education in Roman Catholicism made obligatory on all normal places of education. Attendance at Roman Catholic rites has been made obligatory for members of the armed forces. Non-Roman Catholics in the Civil Service have lost their jobs. Legal marriage has been made cruelly difficult for Protestants, since it has been held that those who were baptized as infants as Roman Catholics have no right to civil marriage; and it is difficult for a Protestant mother in a maternity home to prevent her baby from receiving Roman Catholic baptism. The bibles of the British and Foreign Bible Society have been confiscated more than once, though in the first case some reparation was made. Protestants have been punished for quite trivial acts, such as announcing the time of a service, which have been declared to be proselytizing, and they have been punished for accompanying their dead to the grave. Roman Catholic rowdies have broken into Protestant chapels at service time and destroyed the bibles, prayer-books and furniture, and insulted and sometimes injured the minister and worshippers.

The actual resort to violence has been deplored by members of the Roman Catholic hierarchy in Spain. It has, however, apparently been encouraged by sections of the Spanish Roman Catholic press, and it would be difficult to assert that the general tone of the pronouncements of the Roman Catholic bishops and archbishops in Spain had not made a violent attitude probable. Certainly they have warned the government against any further toleration being conceded to Protestants, and have at times called for greater strictness and, it would almost seem, for no toleration at all.

It is only fair to remember that in the immediate background in Spain lies the civil war, which was one of the most horrible events in modern history, horrible by reason of the cruelties which each side inflicted on the other; and it would be difficult for Roman Catholic leaders to forget the very dreadful things which men on the republican side did to priests and monks and nuns. It is not I think contended that Protestants were anywhere responsible for these outrages, but they were likely to be in favour of the republican side, which after all offered them toleration; and the memory of such events is in any case likely to leave behind a general savagery of attitude which, as I shall contend later on, is one of the burdens of human history. It is also true that the conception of 'Catholic unity' in Spain which is so passionately and fiercely maintained is at least partly political, and seems indeed to be clearly another case in which the passions of nationalism have become inextricably mingled with a conception of Christianity. The ideal by which many Spaniards are inspired is not only that of Roman Catholicism but of Spanish Roman Catholicism containing within itself those values which the idea of Spanish nationality conveys to them. It is indeed significant that Roman Catholics in France and the United States and elsewhere have protested strongly and urgently against conditions in Spain.

Yet this is not a Spanish problem only; there seems to

be evidence that the situation has been even more severe in the South American Republic of Colombia, where Protestants have suffered serious injuries and indeed have been killed in the process of repression. Moreover, it is the reflection of a problem of universal application. Is it right that the State should place all its force behind some particular body of opinion, except in those cases where it is held to be necessary, in order to secure some great good or avert some great evil, to allow each kind of religion to take its place in the State?

The existence in the world of such exceptional circumstances produces difficulties. This is a world of sovereign States in which different religious or non-religious opinions are variously predominant. In such a world it is likely that men who secure in one State that the force of the State shall be enlisted to enforce their opinions will be the victims of such a policy in another. If, where they are, or are likely to be, the victims of such a policy, they make a claim to toleration and equality of treatment, they are in the unfortunate position of claiming a toleration for themselves which if they are given the chance they intend to refuse to others. Moreover, in making this claim they must appeal to principles whose universal application they must openly, or tacitly, deny.

This difficulty was recently handled by Cardinal Ottaviani, Pro-Secretary of the Holy Office in Rome, in a speech delivered in March 1953. He dealt with the difficulties which might arise from an alleged diversity of attitude on the part of his Church which, while it maintained the idea of the exclusiveness of the Roman Catholic Church in a Roman Catholic country, at the same time claimed toleration or even equality in one where Roman Catholics were not in a majority. His answer was apparently as follows. 'Men who feel with certainty that they possess truth and justice do not make bargains. They demand full respect for their rights. On the other hand, how can those who do not feel sure that they possess the truth demand to occupy the ground alone without granting their place to those who claim respect for their due rights based on other principles?' At least that is my rendering of this portion of his speech, which I print at the end of this work.

I do not know how representative this opinion is, or how official; nor for present purposes does it matter. It is not my purpose to criticize what may, or may not, be the tenets of a particular religious denomination, and one which I have had much reason to learn to respect. It is my purpose to consider a point of view; however, as a point of view, if it is to be considered at all, this argument must be modified. It is clearly not possible to base any account of the situation on the argument that one set of men feel themselves to be certain of the truth of their opinions while everyone else is uncertain of the truth of theirs, for that is palpably not true. There are obviously a very large number of Christians and non-Christians in the world who differ from Cardinal Ottaviani but feel just as certain of the truth and justice of their opinions as he does; they are also certain that on important points he is gravely in error. The fact that those who differ from him may differ among themselves need make no difference to the certainty with which severally they may hold their opinions, as from one passage in his speech he appears to believe. It might equally well be said that because there are many diverse versions of Christianity in the world it is impossible for any one group of Christians to be fully certain of their faith in the form in which they hold it, and that would be absurd. As a matter of fact Protestant Christians enjoy a greater degree of agreement about essentials than he has apparently allowed himself to understand; there is unity of faith among the Orthodox; and, as far as non-Christians are concerned, a wonderful uniformity of belief is to be found among the communists; but none of this is relevant. What is more relevant is to consider the results of a situation in which certainty of conviction was held to justify coercive action and the denial of toleration.

The most probable result would seem to be a return to the sixteenth- and seventeenth-century principle of *cujus regio, ejus religio* which helped to cause the wars of religion. When men feel assured of the truth of a doctrine they will deem themselves to have a right and a duty to impose it by coercion on such territory as they control, and if they are conscientious they will believe it to be their duty to extend their sphere of power when they can. It is indeed a dangerous doctrine to launch into a world which is already threatened by ideological warfare and in which communists feel just as certain of their opinions as do Christians. It is true that the danger is mitigated by the fact that a large number of people feel certain of the doctrine of the sanctity of freedom of opinion and the moral duty of toleration; where there is division of opinion there is often agreement upon that, and therefore those who deny those doctrines can yet seek their protection. It is, however, a well-known maxim, that it is a contradiction of principle that freedom should be extended to those who are likely to destroy freedom. Many people are also in agreement on the truth of this maxim; it has in fact been applied rather freely to communist activities, and there would be every excuse for allowing it to affect policy in other directions if the political conditions which Cardinal Ottaviani seems to desire were in the least likely to come into existence.

In the interests of realism, therefore, it is necessary to drop from the argument all talk of the relative uncertainty and certainty of men's convictions. The case for coercive action on the part of the State in matters of opinion must be based on the simpler argument that though many diverse men have sincere convictions only one opinion is right, and that it is the duty of the State to support what is right. This does not avoid the danger that other people may use the power of another State to support another opinion or to discourage a belief that menaces liberty; but it does not evade that issue.

This claim to the coercive support of the State for a particular Church is often put forward in the form that truth has rights and privileges which error does not possess. This form, however, presents certain difficulties. The rights and privileges which are to be conceded or denied are political rights and privileges and must be resolved into the terms of the relationship of one person, or of a group of persons, to a thing, or more probably to another person or group of persons. Truth, an abstraction, cannot exercise rights and privileges; they must be exercised by people in order to safeguard or extend the knowledge of the truth. Similarly it is not to error that rights and privileges are denied: they are denied to people lest they should remain in error, or extend knowledge of their error. The answer which Cardinal Ottaviani put forward to a comparable objection runs as far as I understand it as follows. 'People who are in the truth, who are possessed of divinely authorized truth, have the authority of that truth for their actions, an authority which cannot be claimed by persons who are not possessed of divinely authorized truth but are merely acting on their individual opinions.' However, even granting this premise, this does not completely meet my particular difficulty. Those who enforce these rights and privileges will not be only persons possessed of divinely authorized truth and nothing else: they will also be human beings, and as human beings they will also be liable in certain matters to error and sin. If they can stifle criticism they may use their power to impose an opinion which is not in fact part of the divinely authorized truth which has been committed to them, or indeed to support some policy which is based on human calculations, or human passion; and the probability of abuse inherent in such powers may be of such a nature as to vitiate any ethical justification they might possibly have had. Similarly persons in error will not be persons in error and nothing else: they will also be men and women, and as men and women they will have inherent rights in the eyes of God, which coercive action might violate.

These objections do in fact go beyond the problem of form, and it would be as well to leave the question of form behind and face the general issue. It is claimed that it is the right and duty of the State to give all its support to certain beliefs because they are true, and to use its power to repress opinions which are divergent from those beliefs. For this to be justified, clearly either the State, or those who advise the State, must have had unique opportunities for ascertaining that the opinion to be so enforced is really true, opportunities which it must be assumed have been denied to those who dissent. But it must also be clear that the truth which is so to be enforced must have a special significance for those on whom it is to be enforced. I have had unique opportunities for becoming certain that there are six arm-chairs in my sitting-room, but the matter is of no significance to anyone and I could not claim that I have the right to ask the State to impose this knowledge on the people and to prosecute those who assert that there are seven or five. Religious truth obviously satisfies this condition; it is significant for every man. The nature of that significance, however, has an important bearing on the whole question. If religious truth is to have this importance for a man, he must enter into a relationship with it which is a more intimate and a profounder experience than the ordinary acceptance of an indifferent set of facts. This relationship might be called in religious matters religious belief.

Now I would not presume to say what religious belief is, but perhaps the ground can be cleared a little by listing some things which are not religious belief. The repetition of a form of words through fear of the consequences of refusing to do so is not religious belief. The casual acceptance of a religious system by a man of the world because that is what the convention of society demands is not religious belief. The acceptance of a religious system because it seems to make for security in the secular world is not religious belief. The acceptance of membership of a particular Church in order that a man may get promotion or not lose his job is not religious belief.

With so much I suppose every man would agree. It might perhaps be said that it is unfortunate if the use of the power of the State in favour of a particular religion should produce these attitudes, but that they are a price which is worth paying for the sake of those whose beliefs are purer and profounder. It may be hoped that those who accept their beliefs in these unsatisfactory ways will learn in due course to come to a profounder relationship to them, but that if they do not they will not be the cause of unbelief in others. This is, however, rather a dangerous argument; for to permit a situation in which these states of mind may pass as religious beliefs must tend at least to the formal acceptance of the opinion that they are so, and such acceptance implies a cynical attitude towards truth and a profane attitude towards religion.

True religious belief must, it is agreed, be founded on faith, and every Christian would presumably agree that Christian faith must be gained through the revelation of God in our Lord Jesus Christ. It is also agreed that a knowledge of the facts of that revelation and a realization of their significance cannot clearly come through reason alone. Men cannot reach a knowledge of revelation by arguing from first principles; they must gain their knowledge in some other way, and I would say that there are four possible theories of the way in which God's revelation in Christ is conveyed to man. The first is that it is conveyed by the teaching of a divinely ordained society with an unbroken succession from Christ and the apostles; the second, that it is gained by reflection on the moral needs of the world and on the historic facts revealed in the gospels and in the subsequent history of Christianity; the third, that it is gained experimentally through the experience of those who have tried to live in communion with Christ; the fourth, that it is gained by vision, the knowledge of truth being thrust on the human soul from outside without the co-operation or desire of the man or woman involved. These methods are not mutually exclusive; many men would indeed confess that they had gained their faith through a mixture of these methods. There are also a good many different possible versions of each one of them, for if it is believed that faith is conveyed through a teaching society, there is no logical need to believe that it must necessarily come through a particular teaching society, or a teaching society organized in a particular way, or basing its authority on certain specific historic claims. Alternatively, if it is believed that faith comes through experience, there is no need to believe that it must necessarily come through a particular type of experience.

There is, however, one fact which must be common to all these methods. If a man is to accept the Christian faith, one component in his acceptance must be intellectual assent. If a man is to gain his faith through experience, he must have reason to believe in the validity of that experience; if it is to be given him by authority, he must have reason to believe in the title-deeds of that authority. This does not place intellectual assent in the place of faith; it merely puts forward intellectual assent as something which, if we accept man as God made him, is necessary to validate his acceptance of any truth.

Certainly for simple men and women brought up in a singularly untroubled traditional atmosphere this assent can be largely unconscious. It does not, however, seem to be possible for men to make sure that this unconscious assent shall exist or be prolonged indefinitely; it is a natural condition which can be disturbed whether men like it or not by a very large number of circumstances— by the intellectual development of the people themselves, by the intrusion from outside of challenging facts and ideas, or by the emergence of such challenges from common experience. When this happens, unconscious assent must be transmuted into conscious assent and conscious assent must be supported by argument. This argument will not supply the place of faith. It may well accept faith as its premise; faith and experience may give their full meanings to the words and conceptions it uses. However, argument must be employed, and always is employed. It must be employed, for instance, to show, as far as possible, how faith fits in with the rest of experience, even those results of experience which appear to contradict it. It must also be employed in order that faith can be accepted by those intellectual tests which all men are using on all topics all their lives.

For the whole of human life and society is in some sort based upon argument. It is in part by the use of argument that human beings rationalize the practical conduct of their lives and their relationships with one another. The whole of scholarship, as well as all science, is based upon argument, for argument is necessary for the use of evidence. All philosophy is based upon argument. Even the argument that human arguments are meaningless must be based upon argument, and were it to deny the validity of all argument the result would be absurd, for it would deny the validity of the authority to which it appeals. Of course it is possible to say that it is very difficult to frame an argument correctly, or even that it is impossible to frame an argument correctly; but up to that point at least the power of argument must be trusted. It is also possible to say that argument must take account of experience, that the relation of experience to argument is more complicated than, and different from, what it is often held to be, but that is in itself an argument. Even the most direct expression of the sovereignty of experience, as in the statements, 'I do not understand, I love', or 'I think with my blood', implies the existence of an argument if human beings are to find such statements to be acceptable. The same consideration is true about what it may be held must be accepted from authority human or divine. In fact, to argue that argument is impossible would produce a hopeless situation from which no experience, no authority, no play of logic could provide an escape. If argument were impossible or useless, it would not leave men or women with greater faith or greater logical clarity, or greater respect for authority; it would merely leave a blank in which all would be meaningless.

For this reason all, or almost all, religious teaching is accompanied by argument. In using argument for this purpose men are not accepting an ambitious doctrine of the sovereignty of reason; they are merely accepting men as they are; they are accepting the fact that argument is a necessary part of persuasion, and that the only alternative to persuasion is force, which cannot produce belief. If, however, this position is accepted, a further conclusion seems to follow. The argument to be used must be honest, there must be no attempt to trick the mind into certain conclusions by conscious deceit—a respect for truth demands this, as also does a respect for the persons who are being instructed—and argument, to be honest, must obey certain rules. A fact which might be relevant must not be withheld or denied. An opinion which might be contrary to the argument must be fairly stated and not in caricature. There must be no falsification of evidence. If these rules are not observed, what is practised is, no matter how holy the cause or how certain the truth to be established, not argument but deceit.

No doubt everyone would agree that deceit is wrong, that to use it would be to treat men and women as pawns who could be juggled into believing by methods which the juggler knows are delusions. It is also likely to be self-defeating in the end; for if men come to learn that it is thought they will not believe what is taught to them if they are allowed to consider certain opinions or know certain facts, they are naturally likely to think that the grounds for belief must be in some way inadequate, as the history of many men both Protestant and Catholic who have lost their religious faith goes to show. Yet the rules of honest argument are not easy ones to obey, particularly when dealing with matters which seem to be desperately important. It is natural to feel that the argument must be adapted to the listener, that no useful purpose can be served by allowing him to know of errors whose falsity he is likely to be unable to grasp, though that is a very dangerous line of thought for the instructor. It is also very difficult to describe fairly opinions which are repugnant and seem to be obviously wrong. Yet, so I believe, a creed is normally coarsened and brutalized, and falsified, if it is taught in a perfunctory and peremptory fashion, by teachers who take the easy line of treating adults as if they were children, and who misrepresent alternative opinions which they have never tried to understand, even condescending to the contemptible expedient, of which I am afraid teachers in all denominations have at times been guilty, of blackguarding the moral characters of those who have taught doctrines which they dislike.

Of course it is possible for a teacher whose Church has been granted a monopoly by the State, and whose opponents have been silenced, to argue honestly and patiently and to teach what he has to teach with due regard to justice and charity. But experience suggests that he is much less likely to do so. The fact that no voice can be heard in protest against a facile misrepresentation or a personal libel has an unfortunate result on those who enjoy this immunity; to realize this it would be as well to compare what was said about Popery and Popish priests in England when Roman Catholicism was a proscribed and unpopular creed, and what opponents of Roman Catholicism would say now, now that Roman Catholics have their due rights to speak up in their own defence. And it makes things much worse if an apologist feels that he can, if he wishes, turn from argument to invoke secular penalties, or excite blind popular prejudices. If a respect both for truth and for the human beings to whom the truth is to be taught—and for the human beings who may sincerely disagree—requires absolute honesty in argument, there is really little doubt that absolute freedom of discussion is the best way of securing that that honesty shall prevail.

To me free discussion seems necessary also to secure the purity of the truth in which men and women are to be instructed, though this is obviously an opinion with which many would disagree. To me, however, so I must confess, the point seems to be of the greatest importance. I spoke in an earlier chapter of the danger of the sin of idolatry, of the constant temptation to mistake our own methods of devotion, our own personal beliefs in every particular, for the very truth that we should worship and the undoubted revelation of God Himself. This danger I believe to be very greatly increased if the voices of opponents are silenced.

For one solvent of that habit of mind is criticism, even secular criticism. And here the intellectual history of the nineteenth century offers one striking example. At the beginning of the nineteenth century, religion in Great Britain and elsewhere was gravely hampered by two heavy burdens. The first was a traditional conception of eternal punishment which was incompatible with the justice and mercy of God. The second was a belief in the literal inspiration of the bible. This belief had several unfortunate results. One was the opinion that a Christian must necessarily accept the first few chapters of the bible as a literally exact, or at least an authoritative, account of the beginning of the world, and that a man's faith was in danger if he was troubled, as he well might be, by the difficulty of harmonizing the discoveries of geology with the days of creation, or the sufficiency for its purpose of the cubic capacity of Noah's Ark. The belief in literal inspiration also inculcated the very unfortunate opinion that the tribal ferocities of the earlier stages in the evolution of the religion of the Israelites were moral examples endorsed by the revealed will of God.

All these things were attacked by nineteenth-century thinkers, very often by non-Christian thinkers. Moralists attacked the crude doctrines of hell, the possibility of damnation by chance and the savageries of 'Jehovah'; geologists and zoologists made it impossible for any responsible educated man to believe in the literal truth of the old legend of creation; other scholars revolutionized the whole attitude with which the bible was approached. The gain to Christianity, to Christianity as accepted by all denominations, was immense. Christians were no longer forced to pretend to a belief in doctrines about eternal torment which were a serious impediment to a proper conception of God. The scriptures still remained the oracles of God, but it was no longer necessary to take the old, beautiful and significant story of Adam and Eve as a simple account of actual events to which the results of scientific discovery must give way. Nor was it any longer necessary to take the rather less beautiful story of the slaughter of the Amalekites as an example of the kind of thing that God had in truth commanded.

Yet if ever Christians could have silenced men they would certainly have silenced those who were responsible for these changes. Fortunately in the Britain, and to a large extent in the Europe, of the nineteenth century they could not do so, and God spake also by these prophets. The lesson is a far-reaching one. If in the name of God you silence criticism, even secular criticism, then you are making the claim that everything that you believe, in the way that you believe it, is the direct revelation of God and is worthy of the sanction of the authority of God. To act in such a way is not only to act in contempt of the reason which God gave to man to enable him to receive and judge his beliefs, it also makes it very likely that you will succumb to the sin of idolatry.

There is, however, a much more serious argument against any attempt to secure for Christianity any form of monopoly of utterance and practice by the use of the powers of the State. At some point and in some way the sanction behind such a monopoly must be the use of force. Now to use force to try to compel men to believe what they do not believe is to show absolute contempt for the integrity, the capacities and the rights of mankind. With this men of all denominations would probably agree. In the papal encyclical to which I have referred, Leo XIII condemns the use of force to make men believe. He quotes the words of St Augustine, 'Man cannot believe otherwise than of his own free will.' But if force in the form of open violence is condemned, with it is also condemned the general harassing of a man because he does not accept a particular version of Christianity—his dismissal from his job, the denial to him of rightful promotion or the chance of legal marriage. If any of these things are done with the idea of shaking a man out of his belief, it is an attempt to make him believe 'otherwise than of his own free will', and stands under the same condemnation as open violence, or should do so.

Of course it may be said that the power of the State is to be invoked, not to make men and women believe, but to prevent them from making other men and women disbelieve. Such is the natural savagery of mankind, it is unlikely that the force employed will stop short at what is precisely necessary for that purpose; I do not believe it ever has done so or that it ever will. But suppose that it does so, the sanction behind the opinion so protected will still be force. Now Christians are, I believe, justified in the use of force for one purpose and one purpose only, to prevent the use of force. They are not justified in the use of force in the place of argument. Moreover, for whatever purpose force is used, its use carries its own just penalties. It contaminates that purpose, it occasions cruelty and causes hatred; and the moral arguments against hatred and cruelty must be universal: they cannot vary with the cause in which the cruelty has been inflicted or the reasons which have excited the hatred.

It is important to emphasize this, for men are incurably eclectic in such matters. They are apt to use the suffering of the martyrs on their own side to steel themselves to like savageries against their opponents. This was so in England when men found in the memory of the Protestant martyrs an incitement to the butchery of seminary priests and Jesuits. It is therefore as important as it is difficult to remember that suffering is suffering whoever suffers, and cruelty is cruelty whoever inflicts it; it is as much cruelty to rabble a Protestant minister in Madrid or Colombia as a Catholic priest in Warsaw or Zagreb, for the judgment here stands, not on the type of service which has been disturbed, but against what has been done, or it ought to do so. For to appeal to the general sentiment, or to the moral law, which condemns the infliction of suffering is in fact to condemn the infliction of suffering everywhere, even when it is inflicted by your own friends.

If you are sure your claims are unique, I suppose it is logically possible to appeal in your own defence to rights which you assert are 'natural' and therefore common to mankind, while at the same time you claim that the same rights must be set aside when they impede your own purposes. I suppose for instance it is logically possible for men to claim in general terms full rights to toleration and religious equality in a Protestant or non-Christian country when they intend to deny such rights to non-Roman Catholics if ever Roman Catholics were to gain a majority. I suppose it is logically possible to make a powerful emotional appeal for the 'natural' rights of Catholic parents, their rights as men and women, to control the education of their children in a Protestant or communist country while in principle you deny such rights in a Roman Catholic country to Protestant parents, who are presumably men and women as well. If that is your position, honesty demands that you should explicitly state it to be so, even if that may weaken other men's belief in the force and universality of a rule to which you wish in certain circumstances to appeal. But there is a point where such logic breaks down. The rule against cruelty cannot be invoked in this eclectic fashion, for no man would dare to say that cruelty is odious when another inflicts it but venial when it comes from him.

However, the historic results which flow from the use of cruelty and violence will vindicate themselves on the user with an impartial justice which is rare in the arguments of men. In this matter the lessons of history are worth rather serious consideration. The philosophers of the eighteenth century may have entertained superficial views about the power of human reason, but their motives for desiring to appeal to reason were sound. They believed that to appeal to reason was better than to appeal to the sword. And in this matter they knew what they were talking about. Europe had but recently emerged from the period of the religious civil wars in which very terrible things had been done on all sides in the name of religion. There remained in the eighteenth century much of the old savagery, Protestants could be fiercely treated in the France of the old régime, Roman Catholics intolerably oppressed in Ireland. These things left a legacy of hatred and horror, and memories by which the religion of Christ is still defiled.

The result of the use of the power of the State to impose on men and women various versions of Christianity had not only been that the Christian religion had become sullied by cruel actions: it had also become a mask for the harsh pursuit of secular ends. If a Christian Church depends for its protection on the sanction of force, it must gain that force from some secular power. The force required may very well be liberally granted, but at a price, the price of support in secular matters. It is for this reason that a certain form of Christianity has so often become one of the weapons in the armoury of the secular statesman: Protestantism for the English in their

dealings with Ireland, Roman Catholicism for the Hapsburgs, the religion of Bossuet for Louis XIV. There is
always a danger, as we have seen, that Christianity should
become too closely identified with strong local secular
passions, but this was a peculiarly dangerous association,
for it was too often a collaboration with aggression and
oppression, and with forces that could become corrupt.
It was for this reason that the Roman Catholic Church
was compromised in the fifty years that followed the
French Revolution by its too close association with
legitimist monarchies against which men had real and
justifiable grievances. It was for such reasons that both
Catholicism and Protestantism became drawn into that
horrible vortex of hatred and cruelty, the Thirty Years
War. That is the punishment, and there is no reason to
believe that it will not be inflicted again, for it is just.

For all these reasons it would seem to be of the greatest
importance that Christianity should not claim for its
message the protection of the powers of the State. It must
not sully itself with the use of force or violence; it must
not compromise itself by becoming the mainstay of a
secular régime, for the just penalties for doing these things
are written very large in the pages of history. But
above all things it must respect human beings as God
made them, that is, as beings who are capable of faith
but must give their assent to what they believe, an assent
which it is impossible to force and immoral to gain by
fraud.

This appears to lead back to the liberal principle of
freedom of discussion, but not necessarily to the old
liberal optimism. No man nowadays who studies the

modern scene at all carefully, no man who considers the past with any intent to see more than the surface, can avoid realizing how universal, how penetrating and how powerful are the irrational forces which contend for man's mind. No man who looks into his own mind at all honestly will fail to realize to how large an extent his own opinions are controlled by forces he cannot explain rationally. Some of these he may recognize as channels for truth—judgments of value, aesthetic emotions, the results of religious or secular experience—but he will also recognize other forces which distort his judgment and endanger his character—irrational likes and dislikes, assumptions convenient for his vanity or comfort, the effects of habit and custom—all working under the surface of his mind, where often enough the only evidence of their presence is his feeling for symbols and types. And without doubt a trained psychologist would find much more in him of which he is unaware. Honest argument, free discussion and persuasion may seem to be but feeble weapons with which to struggle with forces so powerful and so damaging, particularly in a world in which the art of manipulating these irrational forces is developing so fast and so dangerously. But those weapons are the only permissible ones; anything else must be employed at a cost which no man who realizes what it is should be prepared to pay.

That fact does not necessarily promise success in that battle. It may be that in the long run the continual discussions and experience of mankind will reveal more truly the ultimate nature of reality; after all, much has been revealed which at one time lay hid. But even if that is so, it will not be of much avail to men and women whose lives occupy a finite length of time; and there will certainly be casualties, people who cannot or will not accept truths which we believe are of the utmost importance to them, or are prevented from accepting them by chance or other men's negligence or evil intention. It is possible that they are likely to be less numerous if Christianity refuses to invoke force to protect its tenets and avoids the danger of being compromised in the struggles which the use of force precipitates. That is, however, only an opinion; what seems certain is that these casualties will exist and present a problem which no man can view with unconcern.

Such casualties are, however, only part of a larger problem which we cannot pretend to be able to answer. Christianity is a religion which claims that certain facts were revealed at a particular time and in a particular place which are of desperate importance to millions of people who can never in this life have heard of them. It proclaims God's redeeming love for all mankind, to a world in which, as far as we can see, the moral lives of very many men and women are absolutely at the mercy of the casual, the uncontrollable and the malignant. But that is the world in which we live; we did not make it, we cannot fully understand its problems. When we consider its casualties, all that we can do is to make sure that we have done all for them that it is in our power to do by those means that we have a right to employ, and no others, and then we must leave them to the mercy of God, the extent and methods of which are certainly beyond man's comprehension. Of one thing, however, we can I believe be sure, for it is taught alike by the experience of history and by the tenets of our religion: the clue to the moral problems of this world is not force; that is why (I speak in all reverence) at the centre of all is the figure not of a conqueror, not of a dictator, not of an inquisitor, but of the Crucified.

The antithesis to force and coercion is freedom; freedom to choose, and to secure that freedom for its subjects is the intention of the liberal State. It is important to remember that it is only an intention and an intention which in existing circumstances it is impossible to fulfil. As a morally and intellectually neutral system of education cannot be devised, so also it is impossible to conceive a morally neutral system of law or a morally neutral society. But where children and men are under an authority which is not neutral, their freedom of choice will be restricted; while if any ordered life, any sphere of liberty is to be assured, the State must exercise that force which is necessary to resist force. Nevertheless, the intention is all-important, important in its immediate results, important as defining the end for which States have their being.

Nevertheless it is important to take the measure of the element in human affairs which stultifies that intention, which often enough makes the intention itself partial and insincere. It must be brought into the account whenever any human intentions or ideals are to be debated. For it discredits all human ideals and disenchants all idealists, or redirects them to less reputable ends. It is in fact the sin of the world, which I will talk about in my next chapter.

CHAPTER VI

THE SIN OF THE WORLD

AMONG the poems of Rudyard Kipling, there is a poem called 'Chant Pagan'. It purports to be the reflections of an English soldier discharged after the South African war. The first verse runs thus:

> Me that 'ave been what I've been—
> Me that 'ave gone where I've gone—
> Me that 'ave seen what I've seen—
>   'Ow can I ever take on
> With awful old England again,
> An' 'ouses both sides of the street,
> And 'edges two sides of the lane,
> And the parson an' gentry between,
> An' touchin' my 'at when we meet—
>   Me that 'ave been what I've been?

And there is another called 'The Return', also put into the mouths of soldiers returning from that war; this is the refrain:

> *If England was what England seems,*
>   *An' not the England of our dreams,*
> *But only putty, brass, an' paint,*
>   *'Ow quick we'd drop her!* But she ain't!

But wasn't she? I am afraid that in part the England of 1902 was just that, 'only putty, brass an' paint', sometimes covering less cleanly materials. So was the British Empire for which Kipling cared, particularly those elements in it which had caused the South African war.

Not altogether, of course; there was much in both that was a great deal finer, but that moment of reaction and disgust either in the returned soldier, or in Kipling, revealed part of the truth.

As a matter of fact, as far as the Empire was concerned the South African War left behind a far more violent reaction than any Kipling might have momentarily felt against England. Indeed, the reaction against 'imperialism', just and unjust, reasoned attack or mere name-calling, spread far beyond the bounds of this country, for it was in large part from an English book published at this time, J. A. Hobson's *Imperialism*, that Lenin drew his doctrine. With that, however, I am not concerned: what I wish to draw to your attention is the moment of disgust, when what has been loved appears clearly in all its mortal insufficiency as something very different from what dream and hope had painted.

This moment of disgust was, however, as nothing to what was to come. Great Britain entered the war of 1914–18 in a mood of high idealism. It was not unnatural. The immediate cause of our going to war was to resist the invasion of a small, relatively defenceless neutral State by the greatest military power in Europe, to suit its own ends and in cynical defiance of the most solemnly attested treaty rights. Behind that action loomed the noisy, bullying power of the old German Empire; behind that indeed there was a complicated diplomatic situation, for whose dangers the responsibility lay more with Austria and Russia than with Germany. Of those issues, however, Englishmen were in the main ignorant, nor do they radically mitigate the immorality of the invasion of

Belgium; Englishmen in 1914 were justified in believing that when they came to the succour of Belgium they were taking arms to resist the naked and intolerable claim of might to set aside right because it was convenient so to do.

Then came four years of blank misery, years in which not only the cruelty but the stupidity of war seemed to be revealed at its worst. In France both sides extended their flanks till they reached Switzerland and the North Sea, and the high command seemed to be able to think of nothing better than of holding men in sodden misery in waterlogged trenches all winter and then, when summer came, hurling them against prepared positions to gain a few miles of devastated battlefield at terrible cost. For the British the climax of misery was probably the autumn offensive of 1917. I well remember the colonel of a territorial regiment telling me of the experience of his battalion when they went in to attack at that time. He was not I think by nature an emotional man, and had had in one way or another rather extensive experience of fighting, but he could not conceal the intense bitterness which he felt when he described what his men had been called upon to suffer on this occasion. They went up all night in the rain, single file on duck-boards through mud so awful that he had two officers drowned on the way up. Some time in the course of the night another regiment, also moving in single file, crossed their front. They had been told that when they reached the position from which the attack was to be delivered they would find a white tape giving them their direction. When they had sorted out their confusions and plodded wearily on, they reached the end of the duck-boards and this position, but there was no tape. All that lay before them was a pathless, directionless sea of mud; and he said to me, when he came to this point in his story, 'All we could do was to laugh, there was nothing else to do.'

At that moment there was a gleam of light from the moon, and one of the officers looked down and saw a portion of the tape where it was not quite submerged. They were able to find their direction and go in to attack and receive heavy casualties. But it is to that bitter laughter that I wish to direct your attention, the laughter in the darkness of men who have struggled at great cost to reach a position from which there seemed to be no road on; for it seems to me to be symbolic of what many men felt at that moment in that war. Men had devoted themselves, absolutely with no reserves, to a great cause, they had suffered more than men ought to be called upon to suffer; and their efforts seemed to have been used up in a welter of prostituted heroism and useless suffering. Meanwhile behind the fighting line much that was ugly seemed to have got out of hand: there was bloodthirsti-ness among those who were in England or in the safer positions in France, and a good deal of blatant noisy insincerity; there was also the tacit assumption of privi-leges by people in comfortable positions, and the making of profit. And when the end came and heroism was rewarded by victory, it was crowned by the Treaty of Versailles.

Much that is unjust and ignorant has been written about that treaty, and it would be out of place to attempt any judgment here; but at that moment it seemed to many people to perpetuate the very things that they had fought against, to reverse the hopes for mankind on which men had stayed their minds in harsh conditions, to promise future wars. On 17 May 1919 the *Daily Herald* published a cartoon by Will Dyson. It shows the allied statesmen leaving the Palace at Versailles led by Clemenceau. Clemenceau is saying: 'Curious! I seem to hear a child weeping', and sure enough, behind a pillar, there is a naked baby in tears above whose head some spirit of prophecy has led Dyson to print the words '1940 class'.

The men who fought through those four awful years were not only professional soldiers, nor only those simple men who cannot reveal their pain, on whose shoulders so much of the burden of history has normally been laid. The armies contained a large cross-section of the nations, and included articulate and intelligent men with no military preoccupations. In the British army there were those who were, or might have been if they had lived and had not been broken by the war, some of the most sensitive and effective writers of their day. It is not surprising therefore that that war developed a literature to whose bitterness and anger it would be hard to find a parallel. The poems of such men as Wilfred Owen and Siegfried Sassoon are not I believe much read now, but they ought to be read, for they are very important and moving historical documents. Perhaps the best example for my purposes is a little book called *Disenchantment* by C. E. Montague, a very gifted writer who fought in the army in the war of 1914–18, serving in the ranks for as long as he could, which was till towards the end of 1916.

He tells the whole bitter story. He describes the enthusiasms of the volunteers of 1914; he says that they had as little about them as was humanly possible of what he calls 'the coxcombry of self-devotion', but that they congratulated themselves on the fine chance that had come their way to do something worth while. 'All the air', said he, 'was ringing with rousing assurances. France was to be saved, Belgium righted, a sour, soiled, crooked old world to be rid of bullies and crooks and reclaimed for straightness, decency, good nature, the ways of common men dealing with common men'; and he quotes Rupert Brooke:

> Now God be thanked who has matched us with His hour,
> And caught our youth and waken'd us from sleeping
> With hand made sure, clear eye and sharpen'd power
> To turn, as swimmers into cleanness leaping,
> Glad from a world grown old and cold and weary.

Then followed the next four years, the misery and horror sharpened by a sense of callous stupidity in high places, a belief that even in the army there were those who were giving themselves safety and comfort denied to the ordinary man, and disgust at the indecencies of the hate-monger in the back areas. At the end there was the Treaty of Versailles, and Montague sums the matter up:

So we had failed—had won the fight and lost the prize; the garland of war was withered before it was gained. The lost years, the broken youth, the dead friends, the women's over-shadowed lives at home, the agony and bloody sweat—all had gone to darken the stains which most of us had thought to scour out of the world that our children would live in.

Montague was probably unjust: the moment of disgust reveals the truth but not the whole truth. Yet there was enough truth in what he said to help to turn the next twenty-five years into one of the most terrible commentaries on the futility of human aspirations that I know. The optimistic catchwords of the war of 1914–18, 'make the world safe for democracy', 'a war to end wars', 'a land fit for heroes to live in', soon became only of use to satirists. A determined attempt was made by means of the League of Nations to reorganize the affairs of mankind on a peaceful basis; it failed, and in the end failed utterly. Many people in Great Britain tried to exorcize war by saying that they at least would never take part in another, and there is every reason to believe that their attitude and the publicity it received did much to make another war more likely. By no means all the folly and crime that caused another war were engendered between 1914 and 1918, or at Versailles; nevertheless, folly and crime did cause another war. Nineteen-eighteen was followed by 1939 and again there came a crisis in which the heroism of ordinary men and women had to save mankind from the lip of almost certain disaster. Then before the guns had ceased to speak a new and grave danger appeared on the edge of the horizon.

I say this not to suggest that humanity is doomed to a series of disasters each more dreadful than the last. On the contrary, it seems very probable that the last half-century was unusually unlucky; it is by no means impossible that a prolonged period of peace may lie before us. If so it is not likely to be peace organized on the high principles and with the exalted idealism with which men had hoped to organize peace after 1914–18. Successful human organization seems very seldom to depend solely on high idealism. Successful management, good luck, a sense of the possible, the power of stalemate—all these things have co-operated to produce conditions which are of great value for humanity, together with more mundane motives such as the desire for security and the hope for prosperity; and what they have effected before they may well help to effect again. With such things as these high principle and idealism may work in alliance, and there is no reason to reject the results.

It is rather of the tragic fate of high principles and personal devotion themselves in a world of conflict that I wish to speak. For conflict is the fate of anything that would inspire or regulate the doings of men, conflict sometimes with good in another form, very often with evil. It is this fact which adds to the sufferings of those who feel most finely and desire the good most passionately, because, however noble the cause, conflict tends to draw it down into the vortex of human anger and strife. This would seem to be so even if the only outcome is peaceful controversy. Controversy tends to harden the mind and reduce charity; arguments become coarser and harsher, and creeds less matters for conviction than weapons of offence, while the motives and integrity of those in opposition become increasingly suspect. But, of course, matters become much more serious when the conflict turns to violence and open war.

The result of war, and of violence, is too often to draw a man down to the level of his adversary; it may indeed seem necessary to sink so low in order to resist him. If he uses poison gas, then you must use poison gas; if he drops bombs on your defenceless cities, then you inflict more terrible devastation on his; if he murders your soldiers, you inflict reprisals. It is perhaps not for us to consider these matters in cold blood without the ugly responsibilities of a desperate situation to shoulder, nor for us to stigmatize those who have had to be responsible for horrible decisions, indeed it is necessary for us to remember by what dreadful methods our peace has been secured. Yet it would be wrong not to see in all this the things which have degraded humanity, as well as some of the finest causes to which humanity has devoted itself. And there is one final and terrible result, that is the development and perpetuation of hatred. If your adversary hates you, it is hard indeed not to learn to hate him, and with that hate are sown the seeds of future evil.

Nor are the causes of anguish only to be found in what is done by the other side. By no means every supporter of a good cause is worthy of it or remains worthy of it. Into all human endeavour personal ambition, the desire for private advantage, personal harshness and pride force their entry and pull it down, and they are often enough emphasized by what is one of the strangest and most maddening of all human afflictions, the curiously strong power of complacent stupidity. The effect of these things is naturally sharpened in the conditions of war when men are being asked to give their lives, but they exist and defile human activities in time of peace. No Church, no religious order, no evangelical revival, no moral crusade has been free from them. They have degraded all that man has tried to do, both what was his best and what is indifferent.

It is for this reason that there comes to sensitive men and women the moment of disgust. They look back at their sacrifice and find it vain, prostituted by others. They look at their hopes and come to believe that they have been so much deceived that it hardly seems to be worth while ever to hope again; and they turn to the object of their love and sacrifice and see that it is so full of imperfections that they can only see it with loathing, or deep unhappiness. 'Awful old England', 'only putty, brass an' paint'; 'We could only laugh, there was nothing else to do'; 'We had failed. . . . All had gone to darken the stains which most of us had thought to scour out of the world our children would live in'; 'Oh! Jerusalem! Jerusalem! Thou that killest the prophets. . . '.

These are bitter moments, and too often they are a true reflection on some of the realities of the situation. In all countries and all political systems there are ugly things which are less innocent than mere 'putty, brass an' paint'. Often enough men have been led into positions in which there seems to be nothing to do but to laugh at themselves and at their leaders. Those who have tried to cleanse the world have not infrequently discovered that after their best efforts its stains have become darker. All Jerusalems have from time to time stoned the prophets sent to them.

These reflections are true, in so far as they are true, because the affairs of humanity are under bondage, the bondage of the sin of the world. I say 'sin' and not 'sins', for I do not know how to divide and distribute the cause of this burden on humanity. The cause for what goes wrong at any given moment is not normally the sin of those who are the immediate agents in it and of no one else. It is often convenient to assume that this is so, but it is not likely to be true. Sin in one man has normally been partly caused by sin in another. Avarice or pride or callousness have been answered by hatred and cruelty, lust by lust and by selfishness, lies by lies, and the moral recklessness of one body of men has often caused the moral degradation of all. The fact that a man is dead supplies no reason why the evil which he has done should cease to be active in the moral degradation of mankind. He goes out, but it goes on.

Such a chain of results can be seen in very crude form in the history of Europe. Behind Hitler lies the Treaty of Versailles, behind Versailles the German actions in 1914 and in 1870 and 1871, behind 1870 are the aggressions of Napoleon and Louis XIV, and so on and so forth. This is of course unpardonably over-simplified. Even were we only to consider the overt and public causes which you find in the history books, the actions of guilty statesmen and aggressive nations, the picture is much more complicated than that; the guilt is clearly much more pervasive and universal, and our own nation is not innocent. We have, however, no right to confine ourselves to overt and public causes. The sins of persons in high places are made possible by the sins of private persons who are their accomplices or provoke them, who create the atmosphere in which they have to act or the situations which they have to handle. These persons may be in the same country, or in another country which in the past may have been guilty of oppression or aggression and so have excited the desire for revenge or made cruelty the custom of mankind. Those who are guilty may have been dead for many years, they may have been forgotten; I have, in fact, little doubt that much of the evil that has come into the world and is now at work comes from sources and individuals that no historian will ever be able to identify. Yet it is constantly being renewed from living sources, and any man now living may be responsible for it. There are no ideological frontiers here; the capacity to endanger the future of humanity is certainly not restricted to those who direct the policy or extend the philosophy of the totalitarian States. It is unfortunately possible that the destiny of mankind was darkened by what you or I did or failed to do, said or failed to say, yesterday; and it may well be rendered still more hazardous by our acts or failures tomorrow.

I think a careful and honest self-analysis will suggest that we are all infected by the past and can easily infect the future. The thing is continuous, an enduring, suppurating, entangling mass stretching back to the beginnings of humanity. Indeed, part of the legacy of violence seems to be inherited from before the point in the process of evolution at which man could be called man; while part, from the very nature of its malignity, can only, it would seem, have been added after the evolution of intellectually and morally conscious human beings.

I want to make quite clear what I am trying to say here, and what I am not saying. I am not trying to suggest a doctrine of historical determinism which eliminates human responsibility. The human responsibility is there and the guilt is there; only, part of the guilt of a guilty action may lie with someone else than the actual perpetrator. A free decision is not just one decision at a given moment; it is a decision in a chain of decisions and it may be impossible to determine how great a control over events any actor has at any particular moment. Nor do I wish to say that the legacy of mankind is wholly evil: that would obviously be absurd. It seems without doubt to be true that 'the evil that men do lives after them', but it is not true that 'the good is oft interred with their bones'. It is probable that each has an equal chance of survival; if it were not so, moral progress would have been impossible. In fact, in the course of the centuries man has built up an enduring monument of good and an enduring monument of evil. Each year he has sown wheat and tares, and each year the crops must be harvested together.

The result is the world in which we live and which in the last resort provides the subject-matter of the great debate and of all moral judgments. It is a complicated world, in which the forces of good and evil do not respect frontiers, political, diplomatic or ideological. They can be found on either side of any line which may be drawn to divide up humanity, and their results may cross such a line, either by the means of attraction or of repulsion, either to gain imitations or reprisals. The lines are blurred and the material we have to handle is alive; the affairs of mankind must always be conceived as a living drama, never as a static picture. The actions of men and their thoughts are constantly changing the pattern of life and altering the moral significance of the categories which we try to use. A political system which appears to be based on the highest principle may become responsible for very evil things through the passions of its adherents or the callous complacencies of its official stupidity. An exalted ideal may as the result of conflict become the vehicle and cause of cruelty and hatred. On the other hand, personal humanity can mitigate the working of outrageous institutions; it might even transform them.

All this makes a moral judgment on the subject-matter of the great debate extremely difficult. It may be said that the solution of this difficulty is to judge by results: that whenever something produces evil it is evil; that an inquiry into the morality of the governments of the world need not go beyond that point. There is much to be said for this test, but unfortunately it is not possible to leave matters there. It seems necessary to go on to try to discover *why* it produces evil results, what historical forces, what ideas produce such results, if only to answer the question how the cause of evil can be eliminated. This task is difficult, but men do not usually shrink from it. In fact there exists a very general tendency to make dogmatic statements on such points, as for instance when men say that such and such an evil is the result of some corrupting political philosophy or economic tendency, such as fascism, or capitalism, or communism, or imperialism; or that another evil is the work of a tainted group like the German nation; or when they trace the source of what is wrong to a man—Hitler, or Stalin, or some other secular opponent. Indeed, even when their diagnosis apparently deals with abstractions it tends to become personal. This is not only the result of thinking by association. It has another cause, for the instinctive desire behind all these explanations is not so much to trace evil to its source in order to eliminate it; it is to attribute guilt in order to punish it.

For this reason it is important that men should learn how very difficult it is to make precise attributions of guilt. If the sin of the world is what I believe it to be, it must be difficult to say that any man, or nation, or institution is wholly innocent of a share in it. But it also follows that it must be difficult to say that any man, or nation, or institution is wholly or precisely guilty of any part of it or, if guilty, guilty in a way that we can calculate or assess. If the effect of sin is continuous and enduring, then it would appear to be impossible to say of any particular agent that this much was the man's own responsibility, and this much derived from circumstances for which others must bear the responsibility. In fact it is possible that the answer to the old question 'Did this man sin or his parents?' may well be that it is likely that this man sinned and so did his parents and so did his grandparents and his neighbours and people in remote countries of which he had never heard. All these people collaborated to produce the evil which we lay to his account. I say this, not to deny human responsibility, but to suggest that it is difficult, or impossible, for human beings to allot it.

Take an extreme case, Adolf Hitler himself. Hitler's actions and personality seem on any analysis to be wholly evil. But how much of that evil was the personal responsibility of the man Adolf Hitler, his own unaided creation, or how much of it was derived from the tone and ideas of the society in Vienna in which he drifted about as a ne'er-do-well youth? How much indeed was imposed on him by all that was bad in the old German tradition? And how much was encouraged by the miserable conditions to which Germany was reduced after the Treaty of Versailles? And who was responsible for all these things? It is probably impossible to answer these questions, but if that is so, it may be impossible to say what was the personal responsibility or guilt of the man Adolf Hitler himself.

This difficulty may be evaded by stating that all conception of moral responsibility must be for human beings a mere legal convenience. It is necessary to assume that every act must have an agent, a machine of flesh and blood which puts it into motion. Adolf Hitler was such an agent; he was the machine of flesh and blood that put atrocious actions into motion. Moreover, from all that is recorded about his character, he was the kind of human machine that was likely to put atrocious actions into motion. It is not for us to say whether it was his own fault that he was like that. If those words mean anything, they represent a calculation which it would be quite impossible for us to work out, and which cannot be our concern. It is, however, our concern to stigmatize, and if we can to punish, certain actions; that is, to prevent or discourage those movements of the human machine that will have certain results, and to eliminate the type of human machine that is prone to them. We do this for the safety of humanity; the rest may be matter for some heavenly tribunal, but we cannot deal with it.

If this line is to be adopted, it should be clearly expressed and explicitly accepted, and it should be made clear that human judgments are not, what often enough they claim to be, a final determination of the whole matter—as it were, an expression or anticipation of the judgment of God. It should also be fully recognized what an incompetent and blundering engine human justice always is, particularly when it is confused by the passions and sufferings of politics. Perhaps Hitler is not the best example of this, for as far as present knowledge is concerned, if he was only a link in the chain of evil, he seems to have been a complete link, indisputably the sole immediate and wilful agent of much that was evil; under any calculable probability, if his personality had been different, much that was evil would not have happened. Perhaps, therefore, it would be better to take a more ancient crime, where the responsibility is more confused and more accidental—say the responsibility of Catherine de' Medici for the massacre of St Bartholomew.

The treachery and cruelty of what happened on that summer night in 1572 can hardly be exaggerated, yet when it comes to the attribution of moral responsibility the problems become difficult. On Catherine's behalf it must be remembered that the moral standards of the France of the religious wars were miserably low, that the ideas of religion had long been interwoven with bloodshed and violence, that all her life had been passed in an atmosphere of lust, cruelty and treachery, that she had ruthless men at her side who must share the responsibility, that she had tried to do her duty for her children according to her lights in the dreadful position into which destiny had thrust her, that she appeared at that moment to be trapped, and was terrified not only on her own behalf but on behalf of her miserable son. The evidence of human sin in its most horrible form was abundant in the streets of Paris that night, but it was not simply the result of the sin of this wretched woman; her guilt in this matter existed, but it cannot be calculated. Yet she used to be painted in the older histories in her relation to this matter in the simple colours of a villain of melodrama.

Catherine de' Medici is dead, Hitler is fortunately dead, and the exercise of moral judgment in their cases is no doubt academic; it may be otherwise when the subjects are alive. In such cases it may be of urgent importance to remember that, while men can pass judgment on an act, it is beyond their knowledge to pass any final judgment on any individual. It is perhaps even more important to remember that these uncertainties increase an hundred-fold when it is a matter of passing judgments on a number of individuals—the members of a class, or a race, the exponents of a political creed, the agents of an economic system like capitalism. Of course it may be said that in such a matter what is in question is not the culpability of the individual, but the fact that membership of a particular group predisposes him to culpable actions. Unfortunately, however, the judgment passed often enough becomes in its form and its results personal. A stereotype is created of what a member of such a group is like, and an individual is hated or abolished because it is felt that he must conform to the pattern. He is a German, or an Englishman, or a Jew, or a capitalist, or an aristocrat, and therefore it is known in what way he is odious and that there is no good to be found in him. He must be punished for being what he is.

In time of war a favourite concept of publicists, which may be taken over by jurists and even by historians, is the concept of the guilty nation. When the rulers of a nation are responsible for the outbreak of war and its forces are responsible for atrocities, there is a strong temptation to argue that therefore the nation itself is a source of evil in the affairs of the world and that its members carry in their blood some form of hereditary taint. Men forget that in order to make even a rough-and-ready attribution of guilt it is necessary to consider, not only the action itself, but other actions which led to it, for some of which in truth men of other nations may be partly responsible. But what is more serious, they may not remember how difficult it must be to measure the moral responsibility or the predisposition to evil of one human unit borne along by a tide which is carrying many millions of people, and caught in an historical situation from which only a man of very strong character could escape. The result is too often hatred and injustice and clumsy generalization, where accurate diagnosis is peculiarly desirable if the origins of wars and cruelties are to be understood, or if there is to be a proper assessment of the inherent tendencies of a people, who must after all remain a member of the family of nations. The problem why cruelty and aggression, or rather particular types of cruelty and aggression, seem to emerge most frequently from certain particular national traditions is a very important and a very difficult one, but it is not enlightened by abuse.

In fact it seems probable that in all peoples, in most cultures, in most traditions, potential good is mixed with potential evil. This is not true of all political theories. It would be difficult to find any potential good in Nazism or, except in a very superficial form, in Italian fascism, but in these cases the evil should not be simply diagnosed as springing from the personal wickedness of Nazi or Fascist leaders, or the fact that they were Germans or Italians; it is necessary to look deeper. But there might be potential good in communism. Much that has been done in the name of communism has been abominable, much that is inherent in the creed seems to me to tend to the degradation of mankind; but it would be absurd to assert that the origins of communism are wholly evil. In its inception, in the passion it can still inspire, there has been mixed from the beginning a real passion for social justice, a desire to right ancient wrong and to secure a more equal treatment for mankind. This element has affected and still affects much of its work, both in its spirit and its result; if it were not so it would not be the dangerous element in the affairs of the world which it is. Moreover, something of its harshness it has inherited from the habits of the Tsarist régime in Russia, something was drawn from the hard practice of the capitalist world in which it was engendered, and something has come from the conditions of its struggle to maintain itself against the forces which have opposed it.

For these reasons the moral issues of the great debate cannot be judged as a simple calculation in political science, as if one could say 'This is a good system: it is the product of good ideas; it will be served by good men and it will have good results', or 'That is a bad system, the product of bad ideas; it will be served by bad men and the results will be bad'. In all human systems what is possibly good and what is certainly evil are to be found; and in their results good may emerge and challenge us where we would least desire it to be found, while what we most value may become degraded till we look at it with extreme distaste. Moreover, in most cases it will not be easy, or even possible, to say from what source the evil which is patent has flowed or is likely to flow.

This does not cancel what has been said before; it does not put all the systems of the world on a moral equality. It can still be said that the institutions and intentions of certain systems of government, or that the conclusions of certain philosophies, are likely to work for the good and freedom of mankind, and that the institutions and intentions and conclusions of others are not likely to do so, even if no precise moral judgment can be passed on the authors and agents of those systems. But it means that in evaluating these systems it is always necessary to take account of the power, the restlessness and the danger of the forces which will use them. In fact it is necessary to consider the tendencies not only of systems, but of men who are all in bondage to the sin of the world.

To do this requires the performance of a task which is different from the mere analysis of methods of government and of political ideas, and harder as well. One of the values of an historical education ought to be that it should be a constant exercise in the task of trying to understand the minds of men and women whose state of knowledge and whose methods of thought and whose values are different from our own. Not all historians succeed in this task, some hardly attempt it; and there appear to exist many ordinary people of goodwill and high intelligence who do not realize that such a task exists. They habitually try to judge other people of different traditions by common-sense rules based on the assumption that their minds work in something of the same way as their own. It seems probable that some of the most disastrous mistakes of this century have in large part been derived from this habit—the mistakes of Neville Chamberlain in dealing with Hitler, or F. D. Roosevelt in dealing with Stalin.

For the sake of accuracy of judgment, as well as for the sake of justice, the effort to reach some greater degree of understanding is constantly necessary. It is a very hard task. It requires knowledge, it requires imagination, it must be done objectively. It is necessary in the work of comprehension not to take sides even when the right appears to be clearly on one side; it is important that the mind shall not be clouded by facile indulgence in the pleasures of moral indignation. Yet it is not probably a task that can be properly essayed in cold blood: not only is it necessary to pity and to suffer with those who suffer, it is also necessary to try to enter into and to understand, if not to share, the emotions of those who may be the cause of suffering. It is also necessary to recognize as far as is possible what are the various chains which have been forged by past hatred and pride and self-interest and mis-conception to fetter humanity, and to eschew the simple division of humanity into groups or types which are 'good' and 'bad'.

It may be a painful task, for it is painful to see to what extent men and women are in the grip of their historical situation, and are cast by history against one another so that they cause each other misery and pain. Yet it is not true to say that to understand all is to condone or excuse all; to excuse all would be to explain away the evil that is in men's hearts, and would not agree with what seem to be on any evidence the facts of world history. To excuse and to forgive are quite different things, yet it is also probably not true to say that to understand all is to forgive all. A wider understanding would probably lead to a greater power of forgiveness than we are normally able to compass; nevertheless, the act of forgiveness is probably different from the act of understanding. There would seem to be no certainty that to understand men's actions necessarily leads us to forgive them, and it seems clear from experience that forgiveness by human beings is not necessarily preceded by understanding. However, these problems are hard; indeed, they lead towards the ultimate mystery, the mystery of the way in which evil can apparently be contained, the way in which the sin of the world is absorbed or, to use the liturgical phrase, 'taken away'. But these are problems which I shall have to face in my last chapter.

CHAPTER VII

THE KINGDOM OF FREE MEN

I WILL start this my last chapter by saying that I wish to leave it as my central assertion that the principle of freedom is of supreme importance in human affairs because in it I see the recognition of the absolute value of the independent actions of individual men and women. Freedom, therefore (I believe), supplies the test by which both the categories of the great debate and the actual operations of the States of the world should be judged; the questions should be, to what extent does some political system represent an intention to concede freedom to human beings, to what extent does a State actually assure such freedom as they can enjoy to its subjects? In saying this I do not wish to suggest that the only States which will pass this test are those in which the subjects are protected by all the apparatus of the advanced Western liberal democracy. There are, for instance, certain stages of society in which men will not enjoy other freedoms than the ancient natural freedoms of pandemonium unless all men are subjected to a discipline more authoritative than the advanced liberal State affords. It is also possible that there are situations in which a man can only reach his full stature by sharing in a common ideal which may not seem to leave much room for private choice and private decision; but this is a dangerous conception, for it may lead to the view that the State, or the political ideal, presents a value which transcends anything actually experienced by individual men and women, something to be realized for its own sake whatever may be the results for the human beings involved. But the true test must be the intention to secure values which shall be individually experienced and enjoyed.

However, the word 'freedom' must never be permitted to stand in any proposition alone, like an august but unintelligible monolith. If the assurance of freedom is to be the touchstone for States and political systems, what stands on either side of it in the equation must be fully stated; and this may cause disagreement. The extreme liberal statement of the equation might be this, that a man should, except in certain specified matters of obvious necessity, be free to do what he wishes, free from any absolute control by the State at all, free to dissent, to object, and in general to refuse to do anything which his own wisdom and sense of right does not commend to him. Only so, it would be said, would he be free from exploitation, from being used as a tool to secure an end which does not concern him. There is very much to be said for this view, particularly if it is extended by presupposing a general intention on the part of everyone to obey in matters of necessity the reasonable demands of the will of the majority ascertained by constitutional means. Unfortunately, however, it is clearly impossible to define what are matters of necessity, and it is also quite clear that in many matters other than the simpler necessities of order and security it is impossible to leave to the unaided judgment of the individual the decision on what is best for him and for his neighbours.

Therefore, if the assurance of freedom is to be the

touchstone, possibly a more universal statement containing a specific statement of what ought to be the object of freedom should be suggested. Perhaps it should be this. It ought to be the sincere intention of the State to enable its members to make their moral choices for themselves when, and as soon as, they can, and to enjoy the values of life as fully developed, freely deciding human personalities; and that they should be, as far as is practicable, freed from any impediment which may obstruct their achievement of this end as independent human beings.

It may be objected that this is to deal in myths, that no such freely deciding human personalities have ever existed or will ever exist. The case would run thus: human beings are always penned in by a number of exterior circumstances which dictate what they shall do, think and say, and these circumstances are so many and so diverse, so strong and so impalpable, that it is difficult to conceive that an independent personality can exist at the centre of them, let alone something which can make any choice at all. There is much to confirm this view: obviously much that men do and think is powerfully affected by their physical condition; we are learning to what extent it is controlled, often unconsciously, by their psychology, and we ought certainly to take more seriously than we do the way they are moulded by their historical background. And when we have taken account of all these things, where is the man? Can he be more than a vortex of contending forces? Is not the only possible truth some form of multiple determinism? If so, the human personality is a legend; its freedom is a dream—and nothing can be tested by an appeal to fantasies.

Against this I would place the fact that so many of our basic conceptions seem to presuppose a power of choice and therefore of something which can choose. The idea of justice, which I believe no human beings have ever really abandoned, presupposes, somewhere, somehow, some doctrine of human responsibility. The idea of morality presupposes the power of choosing whether to act morally or immorally. The idea of love itself seems to me to presuppose the power of loving or refusing to love. These are values which, as far as I can see, could not exist unless their opposites existed and unless there was something which could discriminate and choose, which must include the power to reject. Indeed, the idea of value itself seems to me to presuppose some power of selection and of active acceptance, or of neglect.

I do not mean by this that it lies in the power of men to choose what should be ultimately valuable, what should be true or beautiful or right. I mean that, as far as human beings are concerned, these values do not exist unless they are realized by the free decisions of the human personality. Beauty is not beauty for them unless they freely appreciate it. Truth is not truth for them unless they are convinced of it. Right is not right for them unless they freely choose to do it.

I do not pretend to be adequately equipped to argue about these things, but I am not convinced that the ultimate truth of any of these propositions can be settled by argument. They seem to me to be ontological. They are there, and are part of the experience which argument must use as its starting-point. It is indeed possible that argument may not achieve the task of fitting them logically into the world that we know, but that only proves, what is in itself intrinsically probable, that we know too little about the world and human personality, and that our logic is defective. Against such knowledge or such logic can be placed the universal human appreciation of the nature of value, and that, in my view (and I can only give you my view), is decisive.

If that is so, the test which ought to be applied to a State or a political philosophy can be put more plainly thus. It should be the intention of the State to secure that its subjects should be free from the coercion or the interference of society to choose, as far as in them lies, or to refuse to do those things as individuals which it seems that human beings were placed in this world to do—to appreciate beauty, to understand truth as the basis of conduct as far as it is given to them to understand truth, and to do right as they see the right. To this the Christian must add the rider that this means that they must be free to accept the redemption offered to man through Jesus Christ and to serve and love God and the brethren. Any State or political philosophy which tends to these ends may be accepted; when any State or political philosophy impedes them or diverges from them, it must be condemned.

This, however, leads to the second point I wish to establish. In the modern world there may be a serious danger that any State, whatever its political philosophy, will desert this principle and try to make man in its own image. We cannot do what our fathers could do, and orate about freedom leaving it to the crude chances of an unequally working economic system to decide what human beings shall in truth be free. We must take account of the fact that a starving man is not free, nor is an ignorant man free, nor is the victim of economic oppression; and we have learnt in relation to these things in the last 120 years a lesson which cannot be questioned. In these matters, in many matters, the State must intervene and use its authority to give men the chance of freedom. It has already done so, it ought to do so and it will do so increasingly in the future; and from that fact a new danger has emerged, or rather an old danger in a new dress. It is the danger that it will be the object of the State to create not free men and women but convenient automata, and that a sceptical philosophy, an over-confident and materialist system of natural science, new powers of psychological manipulation and an all-intrusive and very powerful technology may all join to facilitate that result.

We have been warned of this danger, but we may be prevented from taking these warnings as seriously as perhaps they should be taken, because they are usually presented melodramatically. The new and horrible state of affairs is imagined as coming into existence after a series of drastic changes in the organization of society which we know have not happened yet and we may well hope may never happen, particularly in Great Britain with its general good nature and easy-going ways. Consequently what might be realized as a threat is dismissed as a nightmare.

Perhaps we dismiss it so lightly because we forget various relevant facts. For one thing, easy-going ways are the result of easy conditions, and there is no reason to believe that Great Britain will continue to enjoy easy conditions. It may also be relevant to remember that the important changes of history can be gradual as well as catastrophic. They can, they often do, take place silently and unobtrusively without being noticed by contemporaries. What perhaps should be feared is not the sudden emergence of a detestable form of society but a slow change into an increasingly materialist system in which the simulacrum of freedom will continue to be respected but its reality will wither and die.

A melodrama requires a villain, and it is an ineradicable human tendency to look for villains to be the agents of changes we dislike. Philosophers may doubt the existence of the integrated and responsible human personality, but ordinary people habitually go too far in the other direction: they personalize too precisely the evils that confront them. Consequently we are apt to feel that, if things went wrong in this way, it would surely be the work of communists, or of fascists, or of capitalists, or of some undisclosed brand of totalitarian fanatic—odious stereotypes whom we might with good fortune resist. Yet it is possible that we need not look so far afield for the potential enemies of freedom. The most probable agents of change are ourselves and our children acting blindly, moving by an almost imperceptible progression from one position to another, as men do who do not from time to time review their fundamental principles. Such enemies we are much less likely to be able to resist.

However, the most serious impediment to our realization of possible dangers may well be the good fortune of our present position as the heirs of progress. In all probability the liberal State as it exists in the West is, with all its failures, the most humane instrument of government that man has yet invented, and safeguards, more securely than any other, man's independence and integrity. It would be wrong to consider that this condition has been imposed on our society by the irrevocable order of nature. It was not always so: the forces of humanity and liberty have triumphed, in so far as they have triumphed, only after great trouble and some anguish. In an age when the situation is as fluid as it is today and the forces of change are so powerful, the conditions of life must alter continually; they may be transformed by forces as yet undisclosed. As they alter, the institutions of the State will alter also, either in their form or in the mode and results of their operations. Whether after these changes they will continue to conform to the same pattern or protect the same values as they do now will depend on the values of the people who are using them, and, as I have tried earlier on to suggest, it would be idle to expect that our institutions will continue to serve the ends they do serve if such people do not believe in a code of ethics which makes those ends obligatory.

But in the West on the whole we all do more or less share that code of ethics, and it is normally assumed that this code is, after all, the natural philosophy of mankind. Speculation may undermine, discovery may disprove, the assumptions on which it was supposed to rest; but it is thought that no harm will be done, because the ethics we accept will remain as the positive programme for the nations of the world. History does not seem to confirm this comfortable belief. It is only necessary to look into the past to observe intelligent peoples maintaining different and much harsher codes. It is only necessary, for instance, to consider the history of slavery in the ancient world. But, indeed, it is not necessary to go back to the ancient world: little more than ten years ago the Japanese treatment of prisoners of war disclosed what may be done where standards are different.

It may be held that the Japanese are an Eastern people who have not fully accepted the standards of Europe, though it might be hard to explain why it should be held for certain that the standards of Europe will continue to prevail as the positive programme for humanity. Anyhow, there is a more pertinent example nearer home. In the old discussions between the Christian and the agnostic in the nineteenth century, one of the favourite arguments of the agnostic was that systems of belief, particularly the Christian system of belief, were not necessary to maintain the moral standards of mankind. They would disappear, but man, the maker of Gods and beliefs, would rise to ever greater moral heights. This assertion was put, with curious swiftness, to a practical test. For many European men those systems, and their standards, did disappear, but man did not raise himself to ever greater moral heights. Before the twentieth century had reached its half-way mark man in Europe had reintroduced torture, and rule by terror, and slavery, and massacre on a more than Assyrian scale.

Perhaps the argument is unfair, perhaps what has to be considered here is not only the disappearance of Christianity, but also the nature of the type of creed which replaced it; and some form of special pleading might be introduced here to suggest that those conditions were exceptional. Even so, here is an example which must be considered very carefully should there be any attempt to assert that the ethical system which we all favour is the inevitable result of evolution, or the accepted programme of the bulk of mankind, or anything but a particular and peculiar code which requires a particular type of philosophy and system of values to endorse it.

That philosophy must in my view be a non-materialist philosophy, that is, a philosophy above a certain line in the materialist spectrum, which recognizes some objective system of value and some form of human free will. There are various versions of it which may be effectual, but the version of it which appears to me to be true is that of Christianity. I believe that these values are Christian values, whether entertained by Christians or non-Christians, and the sanctions behind them are the sanctions of Christianity. But my beliefs do not matter: it is for you to consider what philosophy you conceive to be true, and then in its name to try to direct, or if need be to resist, the State. But do not be misled into the belief that philosophy does not matter and that humanity can securely rely on some hazily established, loosely defined highest common factor of general good nature and benevolence. That would appear to be a dangerous delusion.

A generally accepted code of ethics, which at least resembles the code to which at the moment we all adhere, seems therefore to be necessary if our institutions are to continue to serve the values they now serve, and to satisfy our test and to guard freedom. There are, however, two mistakes to be guarded against here. The first is that we have a right to look forward to a time when the operations of the State will be replaced by a generally accepted code of ethics, and that that is the meaning of religious faith. The second is the belief that its subjects can gain from the operations of any State all the values that they can gain from an accepted code of ethics, that in fact any State can make men free.

The first mistake is apt to spring from two sources, the yearnings of good men and the oratory of rather thoughtless apologists. When sensitive men and convinced Christians look out on the turmoil and suffering of humanity, the threat of war and the certainty of violence, they are apt to feel that if only men would submit their wills to Christ these horrors would disappear. That is no doubt a very natural and a very proper sentiment; but they are tempted to go further and to believe that the ultimate disappearance of these horrors is part of the promise of faith, and further still, since it is suitable to search our hearts for the source of evil, to suggest that, if our own lives were more Christian and our faith was stronger, these horrors would disappear. This would appear to assume that the possibilities of evil, that is, the capacity for free will, exist in ourselves but not in other people. It is also open to the danger of advancing as an argument for faith, as a bribe to believe, the probability of some future idyllic condition. This last argument is enlarged with heavy hand by the preacher who offers dramatically to humanity through his congregation the alternatives of either accepting Christianity or of being destroyed by the hydrogen bomb.

Even if those were the only alternatives which confronted humanity, that fact would nevertheless be a very bad reason for accepting Christianity; there can only be one good reason for accepting Christianity, and that is because it is believed to be true. No man can believe in the truth of any proposition, or ought to pretend to believe in it, in order to avoid some secular calamity. Fortunately it does not appear to be true that those alternatives are the only ones that confront humanity; if they were so, the outlook for humanity would be black indeed; for who, except when he is drunken with words, really believes in the possibility of a dramatic turning of humanity to God in time to save humanity from the dangers which the hydrogen bomb holds for us in the next few years?

It may be said that if we had sufficient faith we could believe in such a probability and it would happen. But if that is said it would, so I think, show a misunderstanding of the meaning of the word 'faith'. Faith, as I see it, is a realization that, in addition to the existing order of events of which we have common knowledge, there exists another and transcendent reality which without faith cannot be perceived. What the relation of that reality is to the events of our common experience is a difficult and mysterious problem to which we have received no answer, and it seems certain that we overrate the inevitability of the rules we draw from our common earthly experience, and underestimate the power that we might draw from that transcendent reality. But what seems also to be certain is, that we have not been given or promised the power to charm away all the results of evil and sin, either in ourselves or in other people, when these results become obnoxious or dangerous to us. If that had been intended, there would have been no need for the crucifixion, and the process by which the sin of the world was 'taken away' would not have had to be the terrible event that it was.

We are not children playing with life and asking to be comforted and amused by a game of make-believe. We know that we are confronted with the fact of evil in life and with its results. We ought to enlarge our experience of that transcendent reality, the power and love of God, and to increase our trust in it. But we have been shown in one example that, even when that experience and that trust are enlarged beyond the compass of ordinary men, the powers of darkness in other people can achieve what seems to be in the terms of this world a complete and absolute victory. It would be much more pleasant if it were not so: life would be less cruel, more hopeful, more comfortable and more secure; but comfort and security, and the assured hope of comfort and security, are things which we have never had promised to us.

If evil exists (and, for as far as we can calculate, it will continue to exist), it is our duty to take account of the fact; and that means we must use our best intelligence to consider what effects the power of evil is likely to have on the lives of our fellows. To perform this task we must judge the probabilities of each case according to our best intelligence, using the results of such experience as is available. And all experience available teaches that, if an ordered life is to be enjoyed, then the coercive State, with force at its disposal, is necessary to maintain its order. It may be asserted that in certain cases too much force is used, or that it is used for the wrong purposes; and that is a perfectly defensible statement. It may also be asserted that the moral cost of using any force at all is too great a price to pay for an ordered existence; and that, too, is a defensible proposition for those who are prepared to face the consequences which abjuring force will have for themselves and for others. But to pretend that those consequences will not have to be faced is not an act of faith but of fantasy, and is morally irresponsible. If an ordered existence is desired, it seems clear that no code of ethics without the sanctions of the coercive State is, on any honest calculation of the probabilities, going to provide it.

For this reason man may not lightly lay aside the perilous gift of political power, but it is as well to recognize the limitations of its reach. There is an old commonplace of the poets:

> How small, of all that human hearts endure,
> That part which laws and kings can cause and cure!
> Still to ourselves in every place consigned,
> Our own felicity we make or find.

It is not, of course, the whole truth. From many modern instances we can learn what the governments of the world can contrive to do. They can take a man who was happy and prosperous in the morning and strip him of everything before the evening. They can invade the most loving and united family and scatter them to the four winds, so that its members can never even learn afterwards whether the others are alive. They can reduce scholars and philosophers till they are nothing more than hungry men fighting for scraps at the garbage pail of a concentration camp. They can blot out whom they will altogether. These things they can do without the slightest difficulty, as they can also protect men and raise them up and give their life a fullness which otherwise it would not possess.

Yet for all this it remains true that the most important events in the world are probably private events, and all the important results are certainly private results. For this reason the record left by history must be deceptive, since there is so much that is ultimately important to human beings which historians can never record. Historians can record the name, manœuvres and results of a battle: they are not likely to record the name of a private soldier who was killed in it, and they cannot record what he said to his mother or his girl before he went to the war. Yet to those women the fact that he died and had loved them will be the most important fact about an event that may have changed the history of mankind. It is perfectly true that in the generality of its results the issue of the battle may seem to be more important, for that may touch the lives of millions of people then living, or thereafter to be born. But even so, to take effect those results must be broken down and translated into the terms of the private lives of men and women, and must mix and compete with private circumstances and private relationships of which we have never heard and never can hear.

This consideration affects directly the problem of freedom. In the last resort freedom is a condition of the human mind, for it is the individual mind that must make the choices which are important for it. The State may clear away impediments which might prevent it from making certain choices, or increase and strengthen the impediments to others. It may provide a situation and a mental environment in which certain choices are most likely. But in the last resort the decision must lie with the private individual; and since men and women have often enough shown surprising obstinacy in resisting the most formidable pressure, the power of the State may at any given moment be a great deal less than it would appear to be.

If freedom is to be valued, this is to be desired. The object of freedom is to enable men and women to choose matters for themselves, and it is possible that they will do this under any form of government. A man's mind may be free under a totalitarian system; there is indeed remarkable evidence that it can be free in a concentration camp, or even under torture. Sometimes it may be free to make those decisions which are important to it because they are beyond the reach or interest of the government, sometimes it can only make these decisions at great cost which it may be prepared to pay. But one thing is certain: free men with free minds will not be found only on one side of any frontier. The kingdom of free men extends into all countries and nations alike, and we can thank God for the fact.

However, it is not only the coercion of the State which can menace the moral freedom of men and women. In one sense we are none of us free, or ever can be. No one is a hygienically scoured, antiseptically sterilized choosing machine, able to see the facts with objective accuracy and evaluate them without prejudice and presupposition. We are to a large extent the product of our environment, of the traditions among which we grew up, the books we have read, the standards of our companions. I know that it is possible to rebel against these things, but even after the rebellion it is normally found that they have made their mark. Moreover, even if the rebellion is successful, its result in every case is that the rebel has only discharged one set of traditions, of basic assumptions, instinctive attractions and antipathies, to choose another. For these things are the condition of life. The completely detached, uncommitted philosopher is a fiction and to my mind not a particularly agreeable fiction.

These patterns of basic assumptions and feelings can be manipulated in a superficial way by the science of advertising, and at a deeper level by the science of propaganda. To that science much careful attention has been given in modern times, for the force derived from these patterns of feeling has to be organized to produce those large movements of mass opinion which are some of the strongest weapons in world politics today. But perhaps the best evidence for the force of these things is to be found in the fact that nationalism is still probably the strongest single political force there is in the world, for the simple reason that it is from the fact that he is a member of a nation that a man most often draws the most complete and powerful of his patterns of instinctive predispositions.

Indeed, it would seem to be upon the possession by a large number of people living together of similar patterns that a nation depends for its sense of identity. Nations seldom if ever represent races, for, when science and systematic thought are applied to the matter, races are very elusive things; nor are nations necessarily autonomous political units, for there are certain nations which have never enjoyed autonomy and independence; but a nation, if it is to survive, must have as its basis common habits of thought and feeling and a sense of unity which separates it from the rest of the world. It has developed this by the process of people living in close association even when they are, as in our own case, of different racial origins. Thus they develop a common language, common customs, and in due course a common literature, themselves all vehicles of strong unconscious feelings. A nation is also likely to have been fused together at some time by some system of government; it may have developed a more or less uniform social structure, and it is likely to have been moulded by common historical experiences. But neither government, nor social structure, nor common experience, can produce a nation, if the feeling for unity, which must be unconscious as well as conscious, is absent; and that emotion must be based on a common pattern of feeling on which the sense of nationality builds. All nationalities are to some extent legendary, but they must be legends to which something in heart and habit responds.

These feelings go very deep, so deep that they are apt to colour the other opinions a man holds, however universal these opinions may claim to be. I have tried to suggest how nationalism colours religious feelings in Europe today. But the process is the commonplace of history; it is one form of that process by which ideas take flesh which I have mentioned already. An abstract idea nominally valid for all men is apt to become the vehicle of the desires and aspirations of a particular nation, or perhaps a group of nations, and it comes to be coloured and shaped by their instinctive way of looking at things. This happened to a large extent to the forces of the Reformation and Counter-reformation. It happened to the ideas of the French Revolution. It has probably happened to Marxist communism, particularly in its relationship to the Great Russian tradition.

When the promoters of political ideas neglect this element their work is often as sterile and as ephemeral as have been some of the attempts of Englishmen and Americans to export their versions of democracy, particularly to Germany where the patterns of habit and feeling are often very different from ours. It is also probably the same type of neglect that has led to stupidities in communist propaganda, though in other cases they have been able to exploit these patterns of feeling extremely effectively. For it is no good acting as if these forces did not exist, and there is no need absolutely to condemn them. They are probably necessary for thought and action. An abstract idea without flesh is a poor, thin, ghostly thing, mainly of interest to scholars and philosophers and to no one else. It seems indeed probable that it was necessary for Christianity itself to spring from the stock of Jewish tradition; otherwise it would not have been a living creed.

Yet these are dangerous forces. It is often through these habits of mind, normally unanalysed, ill-considered and unnoticed, that the sin of the world binds the minds of men. Most national traditions, most party traditions, many religious traditions, are partially founded on ancient antipathies and rivalries. The memories of 'old, unhappy, far off things', very often in an old, unhappy version of what happened, are preserved through the ages, to continue to distil poison in the minds of men and women. Anyone who has engaged in historical research must have been struck by the fact that very often, after a controversy is over, one party's version of the matter has got lodged in the consciousness of the mind of a nation. Men come to accept without question that party's version of the facts, which has naturally its omissions and distortions, and they also accept that party's view of the motives of their opponents, which is not likely to err on the side of charity. The other party may at the time have made their case cogently and effectively; but it has been forgotten, and they appear afterwards, until historical research can redress the matter, in odious caricature. So the legend remains to add bitterness to party, or class, or religious animosities even within a nation. But clearly matters are much worse when the controversy has been between nations, when bitterness may have been sharpened by the clash of arms and the killing of men, and when the case for the other side would in any case have been difficult to understand, and may never have been known.

It is the task of the honest historian to try to correct these pictures. It is no easy task. His reconstruction is not likely to be welcomed: when one version has sunk to the level of unconscious assumption men do not care that it should be taken from its resting-place and modified. That seems to be an attack on their basic system of values and is painful. It is also confusing, for the new picture is almost always more complicated than the simple black-and-white picture on which they have been used to stay their minds. But the historian can also have no easy task because, if he is honest, he will recognize the working of these hidden forces in his own intelligence. It is a constant struggle and a costly struggle to keep them at bay. His own predispositions, national, party and personal, will be closely interwoven with his own system of values, and there will be an endless temptation to allow the story of the past to confirm them. It is not pleasant to have to record the fact that the wrong side has sometimes been right. Perhaps it is a struggle that no historian can ever hope completely to win, if he feels as strongly about his subject as every good historian ought to feel. Yet all honest historians have to engage in this struggle, for nothing less than truth, justice and the hope of understanding and peace stand on the issue.

But the task confronts everyone, and is difficult for everyone for the reason that makes so many human problems difficult. As ever, the wheat and the tares grow up in the same field. In a man's unconscious historical equipment good traditions and bad exist alongside each other. They are almost inextricably intertwined. The tradition of Israel, the prophetic tradition, what was best in the Messianic hope, were necessary to prepare for what was to come, if other things in the Jewish tradition co-operated with what was evil at that moment to try to bring it to naught. It is no answer to this difficulty for the historian or for anyone else to renounce his national tradition and throw his household gods into the street. If he does that he will certainly destroy the good with the bad. He will also provide house-room for seven other new guests who will be waiting eagerly at his door, and the name of one of them is likely to be personal and intellectual pride.

There is only one road to follow: it is the hard laborious road of understanding. I have spoken of this before. It is necessary constantly to essay the task of imagining what it would feel like to be the child of a different tradition, to be situated in very different circumstances; and it is necessary, as a matter of routine, when considering any controversy in which your feelings are engaged, to think for a moment as carefully and as objectively as you can what case could be made for the other side. It is a task which requires charity and humility, and, as I have said, it requires imagination and knowledge as well. The historians should help you to perform it, the novelists should help you to perform it, and so should the dramatists. Personal contacts should help you. But when you receive any assistance your critical powers must be awake, lest you should be simply fitted out with a new set of assumptions no more just and charitable than the ones with which you started. There will also be many cases where the necessary knowledge is simply not available and imagination cannot supply the defect; for imagination which works without knowledge is only fantasy. In such cases it is perhaps an assistance at the least to remember that there might be another side, that there may be people who approach matters in which you are interested from very different traditions and with different passions to yours, even if you cannot begin to conceive what they are. And you should discharge at once from your service all stereotypes, detestable caricatures which excite your animosity, and all masked words

—'colonialism', 'materialism', or, as an abusive nick-name, 'communism'—which pretend to summarize the actions and motives of very large numbers of people, and which unanalysed have terrible emotive force.

These exercises are difficult ones and they must be done individually. No doubt training can help, and more training in this work of criticism, analysis and comprehension should be given; too much education, particularly historical education, seems to be aimed at confirming one particular pattern of assumptions; often enough this seems to be a nationalist pattern, but when men have tried simply to replace a nationalist pattern by an inter-nationalist one the vapidity of the conceptions produced has normally only been equalled by the conceit of their authors. However, the humility, the reverence for truth, even disagreeable truth, and the critical methods of true scholarship are most useful tools, and a man or woman can be given these. Yet in the last resort a personal effort is necessary, and repeatedly necessary. As always, the road of understanding must be trodden alone, but it leads towards freedom from the cords of inherited and con-stantly renewed animosity, resentment and anger which bind this unhappy world. In fact it leads towards the kingdom of free men which corresponds to no earthly kingdom, is ruled on no special ideological theory and is inhabited by men and women of all nations, peoples and languages—even if some of the languages appear to us, even after our best efforts, to be gibberish.

This, however, leads back to a question I asked in the last chapter: will the way of understanding neces-sarily lead into that kingdom? Do understanding and knowledge necessarily free a man from hate? And is it the only method of approach? One thing seems to be certain: it is not the only way of approach. Everyone with much experience of life must have had the good fortune to meet simple people, usually women, who have contrived to banish hate from their heart and to forgive someone who has behaved badly to them, even though they had not the slightest idea why the offending person had misbehaved. Perhaps this is as well, since some patterns of behaviour remain utterly incomprehensible however urgently we strain our knowledge and imagination to understand them; nor is it by any means necessary that the people who behave thus incomprehensibly should be of a different national tradition from our own.

On the other hand, there are others whom we feel we understand only too well. Unless we are blind or mendacious there are many occasions on which we must recognize that evil is present. It may have been inherited by processes which we cannot trace; but the pressing fact is that it confronts us and it may have hurt us grievously and be preparing to hurt us again. No doubt the answer to that is that we must forgive the agent of evil; but it must be forgiveness with full recognition of the fact of the evil, and that fact puts a tremendous strain on the one who is to forgive. So great a strain is it that a good many human beings have put forward a good many substitutes for forgiveness in such cases. There are simple expedients such as that in *Pride and Prejudice* recommended by Mr Collins as a clergyman to Mr Bennet as the proper treatment for his erring daughter and her husband: 'You ought certainly to forgive them, as a

Christian, but never to admit them in your sight, or allow their names to be mentioned in your hearing.' And there are more sophisticated ways round: there is that bland condescension which is, and is intended to be, an insult to the recipient, and there are those complicated love-hate relationships, which make the act of forgiveness hurt much more than open hostility and revenge.

However, the classical human answer to this problem is to ask for justice. Forgiveness may be possible, but the debt must first be paid. Pain has been inflicted, and therefore pain must be required; that will cut the cord of evil and things can start again. It is perfectly true that the pain or punishment inflicted is normally considered in the modern State to be preventive, to have as its object the deterrence of other men from doing the same wrong, or the malefactor from repeating it. But the desire for retribution is deeply rooted in the human heart; it hovers round every penal system, and provides in all probability its most potent popular sanction. The malefactor must be paid back in his own coin. He has inflicted misery, he must taste misery; he must get his deserts, and in popular melodrama, for instance, he always does so.

Nor is this feeling entirely ignoble. It is often altruistic: men are indignant about ills suffered by others, and it represents a sense of moral reality. But very often the result is not to break the cords of evil and sin that bind the world, but rather to renew them and make them stronger both in public and in private life. Something else is needed, something else always has been needed, to 'take away' the sin of the world. But that brings me to my conclusion, which shall be brief.

I am no theologian, I cannot present you with an account of the various theories about the meaning of the Crucifixion. Indeed, to attempt to consider what it meant as an event of cosmic importance would not have fitted the plan of this book. It was planned to consider these matters from the ground a little way upwards; not from the heavens, or man's speculations about heavenly matters, downwards. Yet, even taking matters from ground level, the meaning of the Crucifixion is obviously so profound that it is difficult, in fact impossible, to define.

And when they had come to the place which is called Calvary, there they crucified him, and the malefactors, one on the right hand and the other on the left. Then said Jesus: 'Father, forgive them; for they know not what they do.'

That last sentence ought probably to be printed at the beginning of all history books, both as a prayer and as a statement of fact. It is not a denial of the existence and power of evil: at that moment such a denial would have been impossible. Nor is it a denial of the pain, mental and physical, which evil causes. To deny that would also at that moment have been impossible. But that pain was not carried over to the account of those who had caused the evil: it was accepted, absorbed and cancelled by the Judge. By such an action the cords of sin which bound the world were cut away.

I cannot tell you what that means, but I can say this. This is not only an event of eternal importance: it is also plainly an example which must be followed. To try to do so requires all the powers that a man or woman may possess—all their knowledge, all their imagination, every nerve that may be in their body, all their capacity for love and all their humility, for they must recognize how much of the evil that is in the world is in their own minds. Using all these things repeatedly and without stint they must ask to be forgiven and they must forgive. The process will not be without pain. Not only will it necessarily involve the humiliating and painful consideration of the extent to which one is oneself a source of harm, as are all those things which one most loves, trusts and admires, but it will be necessary to realize without pretence or evasion the sin and suffering of the world. It is necessary to connect oneself with the common lot of humanity till the mind, like Pope's spider, 'feels at each thread, and lives along the line'. Yet the effort and the pain are, with divine assistance, the way to freedom.

This is not to say that all those earthly expedients which I have discussed earlier which are designed to secure freedom are worthless or of no account. That is not true: they are of the very greatest value to secure that man shall be free from certain specific things to be himself and to do what he ought to do. But they are ancillary: they will not free men from the hate and sin which bind the world; and they are not necessary. Men can be free where free institutions do not exist.

So we have reached the end of our journey, and we have arrived at no pleasant place. It is in fact a place of public execution. Yet all human roads lead here in the end. This is the capital of the kingdom of free men, and there, ruling from the gallows, is the King.

A NOTE ON BOOKS AND
AUTHORITIES

THIS is not intended to be a full bibliography, but only to present a certain amount of reasonably available literature on particular points. It should be realized that this is only a small part of a much larger literature with very much of which I do not claim to be familiar.

CHAPTER I

On the general issue M. J. Oakeshott, *The Social and Political Doctrines of Contemporary Europe*, with a foreword by E. Barker, 2nd ed. (Cambridge, 1941), should be studied; as will be seen from its date, this does not cover post-war Europe, but most of the important ideological issues had been raised before 1941 and it is a very useful reference book. There is also J. L. Talmon, *The Origins of Totalitarian Democracy* (London, 1952), which is only the beginning of a larger work, and subsequent volumes will be more immediately relevant to contemporary problems; nevertheless, as it stands it is necessary to an understanding of totalitarianism. An article by Mr I. Berlin, 'Political Ideas in the Twentieth Century', in *Foreign Affairs* (an American Quarterly Review), vol. XXVIII (1950), is of the greatest assistance for understanding the general approach which men may adopt to ideological problems nowadays.

On communism probably the best single book is R. N. Carew Hunt, *The Theory and Practice of Communism* (London, 1950). A simple straightforward account of communist doctrine may be found in J. Stalin, *Problems of Leninism* (Moscow, 1947).

On the relation of economic and political problems, etc., G. L. Arnold, *The Pattern of World Conflict* (London, 1955) contains important ideas.

There are two useful pamphlets covering persecution in Europe: J. B. Barron and H. M. Waddams, *Communism and the Churches: a Documentation* (London, 1950) and *The Churches of Europe under Communist Governments*, written by a member of the Church of England Council on Foreign Relations (London, 1954). Three pamphlets published by the Catholic Truth Society and the Sword of the Spirit merit special attention. They are *Persecution in Poland*, by Michael Derrick, *Tito and the Catholic Church*, by Michael Derrick (on Cardinal Stepinać) and *Religious Freedom in China*. The first two contain interesting documents. A great many books have been published on Communist China written from a variety of angles, but for the purposes of this chapter special attention might be drawn to a pamphlet, *Law in Communist China*, by Father André Bonnichon, published by the International Commission of Jurists, 47 Buitenhof, The Hague, Netherlands, which should be of great interest to anyone concerned with the problem of the condition of the rule of law in a communist State. Professor C. J. Hamson drew my attention to this.

There are two books on Cardinal Mindszenty: Miklós Boer, *Cardinal Mindszenty and the Implacable War of Communism on Religion and the Spirit*, with a detailed chapter on the legal aspects of the Mindszenty trial by the Rt. Hon. Sir D. Maxwell Fyfe (London, 1949) and *Four Years' Struggle of the Church in Hungary: facts and evidence published by order of Josef Cardinal Mindszenty*, translated by W. C. Breitenfeld and with an introduction by Mr C. Hollis (London, 1949).

An excellent account of the preparation of a political prisoner for trial in Russia can be found in Z. Stypulkowski, *Invitation to Moscow*, with a preface by H. R. Trevor-Roper (London, 1951). On the question of drugs see J. Rolin, *Police Drugs*, translated by L. J. Bendit (London, 1955); it should be realized however that, though the possible use of drugs on accused persons presents a very serious problem in its own right, it does not seem to be relevant to the problem of Russian trials.

On the different attitudes of the Orthodox and Western Churches see an article by Canon H. M. Waddams, 'The Church in Soviet Russia', in *Soviet Studies*, vol. v, no. 1, 1953–4. On Yugoslavia and the case of Cardinal Stepinać see further *The Christian East*, vol. II, New Series, nos. 3 and 4 (1952–3) and 5 and 6 (1953). Nos. 5 and 6 contain the letter about Cardinal Stepinać by an Orthodox priest which I quote with the kind permission of the editors. The figures on Greece I gained from the Greek government, Department of Information, to whom my thanks are due, as also to Prince Dimitri Obolensky, who called my attention to the exchange of letters between the Patriarch Alexius and Damaskinos, Archbishop of Athens. The original version of the Archbishop's letter can be found in the Athens periodical *Ekklesia* for 15 July 1948, pp. 209–10.

CHAPTERS IV AND V

For the discussion of the problem of freedom as it stands at the moment the student is probably best referred to Maurice Cranston, *Freedom. A new analysis* (London, 1953) and Professor Gilbert Ryle, *The Concept of Mind* (London, 1951). There is a helpful description of the various modern schools of philosophy in *Contemporary Philosophy*, by Frederick Copleston, S.J. (London, 1956). Every educated man should have read John Stuart Mill *On Liberty* (any edition), and it is very well worth while to read Sir James Fitzjames

Stephen's commentary on Mill's ideas in *Liberty, Equality and Fraternity* (London, 1874).

The quotation from Stalin comes from his account of 'Dialectical and Historical Materialism' in *Problems of Leninism* (Moscow, 1947), p. 576.

For Leo XIII's Encyclical Letter on the Christian Constitution of States, *Immortale Dei*, see *Acta Sanctae Sedis*, vol. XVIII, pp. 161 ff. (Rome, 1885). The Latin text with an authorized translation was published in London in 1886.

On Spain probably the best book is J. D. Hughey Jr., *Religious Freedom in Spain, its Ebb and Flow* (London, 1955). It should be noted that it is from the Protestant side; another book from the same side is Jacques Delpech, *The Oppression of Protestants in Spain* (Boston, 1955), as is also *Religious Liberty in Peril. Documents illustrating the condition of Protestants in Spain* (Paris, 1948), which contains some useful documents. The British Council of Churches, 39 Doughty Street, London, W.C.1, and The Evangelical Alliance (Overseas Dept.), 39 Ladbroke Grove, Holland Park, London, W.11, and the Evangelical Alliance of Colombia have issued bulletins on the situation in Colombia in South America.

On the fierceness of the Spanish civil war see Georges Bernanos, *Les Grands cimetières sous la lune* (Paris, 1938).

CHAPTER VI

Disenchantment by C. E. Montague was first published in 1922. It was later published in the Phoenix Library by Messrs Chatto and Windus.

I have to thank my brother, Commander E. Bidder Clark, for calling my attention to the prophetic cartoon by Will Dyson and to the *Daily Herald* Editorial Office for identifying and dating it for him. It is published in *The Kemsley Manual of Journalism*.

REPORT OF SPEECH BY
CARDINAL OTTAVIANI

Taken from *Osservatore Romano*, 4 March 1953

(See chapter v, page 135)

Nella sua esposizione — densa di dottrina, di riferimenti storici e di applicazioni alle necessità dell'oggi — l'Em.mo Cardinale Ottaviani intende esprimere un omaggio all'alto e luminoso insegnamento del Sommo Pontefice Pio XII, il Quale, nell'attuazione fedele del Magistero affidato da Cristo alla sua Chiesa, continua, con apostolica fermezza, l'opera provvidenziale dei Successori di Pietro.

Si sono affacciate in questi ultimi tempi, pur fra cattolici, delle errate valutazioni circa i poteri esistenti nella Chiesa, cioè di ordine e di giurisdizione. Taluni sostengono che il primo andrebbe sempre più affievolendosi a vantaggio del secondo: il che porterebbe ad una grande innovazione nella primitiva disciplina ecclesiastica.

L'Em.mo ha rivendicato alla Chiesa il suo carattere di *società perfetta*, con tutti i poteri inerenti a tale condizione giuridica, per svolgere la sua missione in ogni Stato, senza contrasti delle Società, di cui Dio è, in diverso modo, autore e sostenitore.

Sorge il problema della convivenza della Chiesa con lo Stato laico. Anche qui alcune teorie recenti sono da riprovarsi o per lo meno sono inesatte. V'è chi sostiene, ad esempio, che nel complesso dell'insegnamento della Chiesa occorre distinguere una parte permanente e una caduca, dovuta, quest'ultima, al riflesso di particolari condizioni temporanee. Ed ecco il Santo Padre Pio XII ammonire, nella *Humani generis*, che dobbiamo accettare nelle Encicliche il magistero ordinario della Chiesa: ed in questo Egli ribadische quanto già è stato asserito dai Sommi Pontefici, segnatamente nei tempi a noi più vicini, da Leone XIII nella Enciclica *Immortale Dei*.

L'Em.mo Cardinale Ottaviani ha quindi toccato il problema della confessionalità di uno Stato cattolico e delle relative conseguenze di fronte ai culti non cattolici.

Verità certa e indiscutibile tra i principii del Diritto Pubblico Ecclesiastico, è quella del dovere dei Governanti, in uno Stato composto nella quasi totalità da cattolici e, conseguentemente e coerentemente, retto da cattolici, di informare la legislazione in senso cattolico. Il che importa tre immediate conseguenze: (1) la professione sociale e non soltanto privata della Religione del popolo; (2) la ispirazione cristiana della legislazione; (3) la difesa del patrimonio religioso del popolo contro ogni assalto di chi vorrebbe strappare ad esso il tesoro della fede e della sua pace religiosa.

L'Em.mo Oratore ha spiegato, sempre con l'appoggio degli odierni Documenti pontifici, questa triplice verità, rilevando altresì come in essi vi sia constante armonia e linearità di dottrina.

A tale proposito, dopo aver fatto appello alla *Immortale Dei*, di Leone XIII, l'Em.mo Cardinale si è richiamato alla *Summi Pontificatus* di Pio XII. Egli ha rilevato la fermezza e l'immobilità dei principi della Chiesa, citando, inoltre, le Encicliche *Libertas* e *Sapientiae christianae* di Leone XIII, le Encicliche di Pio XI *Divini Redemptoris* contro il comunismo, *Mit brennender Sorge* contro il nazismo, e *Non abbiamo bisogno* contro il monopolio statale del fascismo.

In questa medesima luce egli poi risolve una difficoltà spesso presentata, ai nostri tempi: quella circa un presunto diverso atteggiamento della Chiesa, la quale, mentre in un paese cattolico sostiene l'idea della protezione esclusiva della religione cattolica, in altri paesi, ove i cattolici sono minoranza, reclama il diritto alla tolleranza o addirittura alla parità dei culti. La risposta è chiarissima. 'Gli uomini che si sentono nel sicuro possesso della verità e della giustizia, non vengono a transazioni. Essi esigono il pieno rispetto dei loro diritti. Coloro invece che non si sentono sicuri del possesso della verità, come possono esigere di tener soli il campo, senza far parte a chi reclama il rispetto dei propri diritti in base ad altri principii?'

Ad esempio come si può mettere sulla base di una presunta parità la Chiesa Cattolica e le 146 confessioni protestantiche che, nelle riunioni di Amsterdam nel 1949, non trovarono neppure un punto di accordo sostanziale?

Il riconoscimento dei diritti di Dio e della Chiesa non è affatto inconciliabile con la civiltà moderna: per fare il suo dovere un Governante cattolico d'uno Stato cattolico non ha bisogno di essere un assolutista, nè di tornare al complesso della civiltà del Medio Evo.

Sempre a proposito del pluralismo religioso, l'Em.mo Oratore ha confutato un altro principio da respingere, oggi asserito, e cioè che nè l'errore, nè la verità, che sono delle astrazioni, vanno considerate oggetto di diritto.

I diritti in questione, invece, sono ottimamente subiettati negli individui che sono nella verità: eguali diritti non possono esigere gli individui a titolo del loro errore. Ora nelle Encicliche ricordate il primo soggetto di questi diritti è proprio Iddio: dal che consegue che sono nel vero diritto soltanto coloro che obbediscono ai suoi mandati e si trovano nella sua verità e nella sua giustizia.

L'Em.mo Cardinale Ottaviani, quali argomenti pratici in aggiunta alla sua esposizione, non manca di citare esempi eloquenti nei comportamenti di quelli che, mentre accentuano critiche verso la legislazione d'uno Stato cattolico, non dimostrano affatto il medesimo zelo quando si tratta, poniamo, delle costituzioni di Stati a regime comunista; e nel rilevare quanto di ingiusto esista ancora nelle leggi di vari Stati, pure cristiani, dell'Europa e delle Americhe. Da ciò risulta come stridente sia il levare protesta a carico di uno Stato contro taluni provvedimenti di legittima difesa, mentre in casa propria non mancano fatti analoghi di ostracismi e di espulsioni.

L'Em.mo Porporato ha concluso il suo discorso illustrando il mandato divino della Chiesa ad esercitare la sua azione nella società, in tutti i campi della umana attività, senza eccezione alcuna, come, con altezza di concetti e vigore di espressioni, affermava il Sommo Pontefice Pio XII nella Allocuzione ai Parroci di Roma nel marzo del 1946.

Quel mandato la Chiesa sigilla con il suo sangue, sparso nei campi di concentramenti, nelle prigioni, tra i martirii fisici e spirituali, il cui valore per la Chiesa Pio XII ha più volte mirabilmente esaltato.

The French Translation can be found in *L'Osservatore Romano, Édition Hebdomadaire en Langue Française*, quatrième année, No. 11 (169), 13 March 1953. The passage translated in the Text of Chapter V runs thus: 'Les hommes qui sentent avec certitude posséder la vérité et la justice ne se livrent pas à des transactions. Ils exigent le plein respect de leurs droits. En revanche ceux qui ne se sentent pas sûrs de posséder la vérité, comment peuvent-ils exiger de tenir le terrain à eux seuls, sans accorder leur part à ceux qui réclament le respect de leurs propres droits basés sur d'autres principes?'